Everett Ruess, ca. 1932–1933

CANYON de CHELLY

Edgar Payne, *Blue Canyon,* 1920s. Oil on canvas, 34 x 34 inches. Private collection.
Photograph courtesy of George Stern Fine Arts.

Places of Spirit Series

CANYON de CHELLY

100 years of painting and photography

Donald J. Hagerty

SALT LAKE CITY

First Edition
99 98 97 96   5 4 3 2 1

This is a Peregrine Smith Book, published by
Gibbs Smith, Publisher
P.O. Box 667
Layton UT 84041

Design by Leesha Jones
Printed in Hong Kong

Library of Congress Cataloging-in-Publication Data

Hagerty, Donald J.
Canyon de Chelly : 100 Years of Painting and Photography / by Donald J. Hagerty.
p.   cm.
"Peregrine Smith Books"—
Includes bibliographical references and index.
ISBN 0-87905-705-X
1. Chelly, Canyon de (Ariz.) in art. 2. Canyon de Chelly National
    Monument (Ariz.)—Pictorial works. 3. Art, American. 4. Art,
    Modern—20th century—United States. I. Title.
N8214.5.U6H24   1996
758'.179137—dc20   95-53676
                        CIP

CONTENTS

Chronology of Painters and Photographers at
Canyon de Chelly, 1849–1945 6

Acknowledgments 8

Introduction 9

Among the Rocks, 1849–1900 17

A Far-Off Place, 1900–1920 31

Time and Culture, 1920–1945 58

Landscape of the Heart, 1945–Present 85

Bibliography 120

CHRONOLOGY OF PAINTERS AND PHOTOGRAPHERS AT CANYON DE CHELLY, 1849–1945

1849
Richard H. Kern (1821–1853)
   Painter
Edward M. Kern (1823–1863)
   Painter

1859
Joseph Heger (1835–1897)
   Painter, Lithographer

1873
Timothy O'Sullivan (1840–1882)
   Photographer
Alexander H. Wyant (1836–1892)
   Painter

1877
John Dare Howland (1843–1914)
   Painter

1879
John K. Hillers (1843–1925)
   Photographer

1881
John K. Hillers

1882
John K. Hillers
Ben Wittick (1845–1903)
   Photographer

1883
Cosmos Mindeleff (?)
   Ethnologist, Photographer

1885
Ben Wittick
Cosmos Mindeleff

1890
Ben Wittick

1893
Cosmos Mindeleff

1897
Ben Wittick

1899
Arnold Genthe (1869–1942)
   Photographer
Frederick I. Monsen (1865–1929)
   Photographer

1900
Sumner W. Matteson (1867–1920)
   Photographer
Frank Russell (1868–1903)
   Ethnologist, Photographer

1902
Maynard Dixon (1875–1946)
   Painter
Stewart Culin (1858–1929)
   Ethnologist, Photographer
Ben Wittick
Frederick I. Monsen

1903–1905
Simon Schwemberger (1867–1931)
   Photographer

1903
Ben Wittick
C. B. Lang (?)
   Photographer
Herbert B. Judy (1874–1946)
   Painter

1904
John W. Norton (1876–1934)
   Painter
Edward S. Curtis (1868–1952)
   Photographer
Adam Clark Vroman (1856–1916)
   Photographer
Maynard Dixon

1905
Maynard Dixon

1906
Charles F. Lummis (1859–1928)
   Photographer
Frederick H. Maude (1858–1960)
   Photographer
Edward S. Curtis

1907
Elbridge Ayer Burbank (1858–1949)
   Painter

1908
Louis B. Akin (1868–1913)
   Painter
Frederick I. Monsen

1909
Francis J. McComas (1875–1938)
   Painter
Carl Moon (1878–1949)
   Photographer, Painter

1910
Ferdinand Burgdorff (1881–1975)
   Painter

1912
Alonzo Megargee (1883–1960)
  Painter
Emry Kopta (1884–1953)
  Sculptor, Painter
William R. Leigh (1866–1955)
  Painter
Louis Akin

1913
Roland Reed (1864–1934)
  Photographer

1914
Francis J. McComas

1915
Maynard Dixon

1916
Carl Oscar Borg (1879–1947)
  Painter, Etcher
Edgar Payne (1883–1947)
  Painter
C. Bertram Hartman (1882–1960)
  Painter
William R. Leigh

1917
C. Bertram Hartman
Edward Borein (1873–1945)
  Painter, Etcher
Carl Oscar Borg
Sheldon Parsons (1866–1943)
  Painter

1918
Carl Oscar Borg
Emry Kopta

1919
Sheldon Parsons
Herbert F. Robinson (1865–1956)
  Photographer

1919 Continued
Gerald Cassidy (1869–1934)
  Painter

1920–1940
Edgar Payne

1920–1932
Carl Oscar Borg

1920
Joseph R. Willis (1876–?)
  Painter, Photographer

1922
Maynard Dixon

1923
Maynard Dixon
Emry Kopta
Earl Morris (1891–1956)
  Archaeologist, Photographer
Ann Morris (?)
  Painter, Photographer
Laura Adams Armer (1874–1963)
  Painter, Photographer

1925
Hansen Duvall Puthuff (1875–1972)
  Painter
George Townsend Cole (1874–1937)
  Painter

1927
Raymond Jonson (1891–1982)
  Painter

1929–1930
Gordon Coutts (1868–1937)
  Painter

1930
Laura Gilpin (1891–1979)
  Photographer
Alonzo Megargee

1932
George A. Grant (1891–1964)
  Photographer

1932–1934
Everett Ruess (1914–1934)
  Painter

1934
George A. Grant

1935
George A. Grant

1937
Ansel Adams (1902–1984)
  Photographer
William R. Leigh
Ethel Traphagen Leigh (1883–1963)
  Painter
Conrad Buff (1886–1975)
  Painter

1939
Gina Knee (1898–1982)
  Painter
W. Langdon Kihn (1898–1957)
  Painter

1940
Ralph H. Anderson (?)
  Photographer
George A. Grant

1941–1942
Ansel Adams

1943
Gerald Curtis Delano (1890–1972)
  Painter

ACKNOWLEDGMENTS

Numerous individuals helped with this book, all of them partners in a creative process. As usual, my family is always an integral part of these endeavors. My wife, Rebecka, helped in countless ways, and her presence graces these pages.

Chauncey Neboyia introduced me to Canyon de Chelly via Bare Trail in the early 1980s, a marvelous hike down from the rim of Canyon del Muerto, forever downward, it seemed, into the Canyon's past—and present. Chauncey's links to the past, including his work with Earl Morris, vastly increased my appreciation of a magical, mystical landscape. The climb back up Bare Trail to Canyon del Muerto's rim on a hot August afternoon was also unforgettable. Stephen Jett, Professor of Geography, University of California–Davis, volunteered his formidable knowledge of Canyon de Chelly, which included suggestions for artists, identification of specific canyon locations represented in paintings and photographs, and Navajo culture.

Many of the contemporary artists profiled in this book shared thoughts about their work, contributed examples of photographs or paintings, discussed Canyon de Chelly's impact on their art, and otherwise helped shape contours of the book. Ed Mell, Bill Schenck, Wilson Hurley, Woody Gwyn, Lindsay Holt II, Alyce Frank, Barbara Zaring, Lynn Taber-Borcherdt, Peter Holbrook, Brooks Anderson, Merrill Mahaffey, and Charles Fritz have added their contributions to the visual history of Canyon de Chelly.

Shirley Harding, Park Curator at Hubbell Trading Post National Historic Site, Ganado, Arizona, was most helpful on my visit there and throughout the project. Tara Travis, Park Historian, and Scott Travis, Park Archaeologist, Canyon de Chelly National Monument, read the text. Their comments and suggestions are gratefully acknowledged.

Numerous art dealers and galleries offered suggestions about prospective artists, tracked down paintings or photographs, and facilitated contacts with their clients. Museums and other organizations have been most helpful with loans of photographs and information about painters and photographers.

Fig. 1
Wilson Hurley, *Winter Sunset, de Chelly*, 1977. Oil on canvas, 40 x 72 inches. Courtesy of the artist.

INTRODUCTION

There are thousands of canyons in the Southwest, from the Grand Canyon to Chaco Canyon, to ones whose names have been forgotten, even nameless ones. But perhaps none in this lithic land possesses the spiritual, sacred feel of Canyon de Chelly in northeast Arizona. Some canyons assumed their names from a historical event, description of unusual beauty, or specific topographical features. But Canyon de Chelly stands apart, a landscape of the heart. And different, as light plays with radiance on great red sandstone walls, agitated cottonwood leaves rattle and rotate in the slightest wind, voices of Navajo in the canyon echo up through time, and timeless silence hovers over all. Centuries whisper from the canyon's walls, mute testimony about the agelessness of this land (figure 1).

Canyon de Chelly, a national monument since 1931, is located on the Navajo Reservation, just east of Chinle, Arizona. Characterized by vertical red sandstone walls that thrust up from the canyon bottom like great cathedrals, Canyon de Chelly and its major tributary, Canyon del Muerto, were cut deep into rock by rushing streams from the nearby Chuska Mountains. Over time, these acrobatic watercourses created an alchemy of twists, curves, and coils that left slickrock walls sometimes a thousand feet above the narrow canyon floor. In certain places, canyon walls are smooth and uniform; in other areas, ledges, fissures, overhangs, cracks or cross-bedded forms intersect the flow of rock monoliths. Contorted swirls of cross-bedded sandstone (in particular, remains of ancient

Fig. 2
Carl Oscar Borg, *Canyon de Chelly,* 1925. Oil on canvas.
Collection of John Villadsen. Photograph courtesy
of Helen Laird.

sand dunes), have weathered into irregular and expressive formations of vermilion rock. Passage is traced in places by serpentine views of the cobalt blue sky above. In Canyon del Muerto, the great walls edge even closer together, undercut but twisted together, seemingly, by even thinner trace of sky. The Navajo name for the canyon, Tseyi', translated as "canyon" or "among the rocks," eventually became Hispanicized and Anglicized into Canyon de Chelly; but "among the rocks" remains an accurate term for this sculpted canyon system, for rock is the dominant feature (figure 2).

Canyon de Chelly has been occupied almost continuously for nearly twenty centuries. While the canyon's natural beauty ranks it among the West's major landmarks, its status as one of the greatest concentrations of prehistoric cliff dwellings and rock art in the Southwest has excited generations of photographers and painters. Antelope House, Mummy Cave, White House Ruin, and Big Cave are just several spectacular sites among more than seven hundred ruins scattered throughout Canyon de Chelly and Canyon del Muerto. The Navajo called them *tse yaa kin,* "houses beneath the rock." Remote, inscrutable, the cliff ruins impart an excitement for the distant past and have touched all who view them, much as Willa Cather expressed:

> Far up above me, a thousand feet or so, set in a great cavern in the face of the cliff, I saw a little city of stone asleep. It was as still as sculpture—and something like that. It all hung together, seemed to have a kind of composition: pale little houses of stone nestling close to one another, perched on top of each other, with flat roofs, narrow windows, straight walls, and in the middle of the group, a round tower.

> In sunlight it was the color of winter oak leaves. A fringe of cedars grew along the edge of the cavern, like a garden. They were the only living things. Such silence and stillness and repose—immortal repose. That village sat looking down into the canyon with the calmness of eternity. I had come upon the city of some extinct civilization, hidden away in this inaccessible mesa for centuries, preserved in the dry air and almost perpetual sunlight like a fly in amber, guarded by the cliffs and the river and the desert.

> —WILLA CATHER, *The Professor's House*

The Anasazi, named with a Navajo word that means "ancestral enemies," occupied much of the Southwest's Colorado Plateau from circa A.D. 300 to about A.D. 1300, their settlements often located in shallow alcoves set into sandstone walls, as at Canyon de Chelly. Built of material from the land, their long-vacant homes merge with the natural scene. Sometimes, as at White House Ruin, morning light that recoils from canyon walls illuminates the structure like a boxed jewel. The sweep of canyon walls envelops this graveyard of human-erected architecture, a gigantic swirl of water and wind-shaped red sandstone (figure 3).

Canyon de Chelly has a long, rich history of art and has exerted a profound, even spiritual influence on people who lived there, and on artists, past and present, attracted by the magnificent beauty of sandstone passages. The first artists used neither canvas nor paper but sandstone, and painted, pecked, or incised an infinite variety of symbolic and representational forms on the smooth surface of canyon walls. A magnificent repository of Anasazi stick figures—large, abstract anthropomorphic forms, avian and quadruped forms, handprints, a variety of geometric designs, and human figures, including Kokopelli, the flute player—are found on walls throughout the canyon. Early inhabitants of the canyon were concerned with spirit powers, and the primordial abstraction of their rock art reveals a complex symbolic and metaphoric universe.

When the Navajo arrived at Canyon de Chelly in the mid-1700s, they added their own visual interpretations drawn from the world around them. Like the Anasazi before, the Navajo began to paint and draw and, more rarely, incise images on canyon walls. From the late eighteenth to the early nineteenth century, the Navajo depicted their ceremonial images with abstract stylization. In time, the Navajo portrayed secular subjects—horses, antelope, cattle, explorers, conflicts—in a realistic and dynamic manner.

In the mid-nineteenth century, new artists arrived at Canyon de Chelly, members of scientific and military expeditions sent to investigate unknown territory after Mexico ceded a large block of the Southwest to the United States at the Mexican War's conclusion. This was an issue of nascent Manifest Destiny at first, followed by an explosive era of great government surveys, scientific exploration, and, during the 1870s and 1880s, extensive inventory of what existed in the American West.

As the twentieth century opened, more artists began to make the long, difficult journey to Canyon de Chelly, attracted by stories of dramatic landscapes and colorful Navajo. But even from the 1920s to the 1940s, visitors to the canyon were few, intimidated by crude, almost nonexistent roads and long distances. Some artists ventured into Canyon de Chelly only once while others returned numerous times. All were touched by the canyon's scale, light, color, and a con-sciousness of long human history. They have left a pictorial legacy of impressions, their meditations on an ancient landscape. One of them, Maynard Dixon, who first explored Canyon del Muerto in 1902, later recalled his thoughts:

Walls of the wonderful canyon-red walls of sun-tinted sandstone, where little winds pass and the pale sand drifts at the base of enormous slabs…Sheer walls, grand amphitheaters, turrets, ledges and domes— twists of hollow shadows between revela-tion of sun—and there the beginning of arches, split off from the lightning-scarred rock of a thousand year silence; to be, at the end of another ten-thousand year silence, a cavern to hold the dim records of men yet predated. There, so the Navajo say, the ghosts of Yei-Bechai, abide in the cliff-dwellers ruins, where they glide between sunlight and shadow.

There, high on the walls, unnamed, undeciphered, are graven the symbols of tribes long since sifted away into the dust of the desert—the mysterious giant ancestors, dimly remembered. There, as the war-eagle sails slowly along the sky-brink, his blue shadow slants far down the immense broken red fingers of stone. Close-grouped the few cottonwoods stand, green in the cove of the canyon, where the sand-bars are hard and damp from the freshet; and near, is the rain-carven waterhole, glimmer the little pool, blue to the sky. Then a thin sound, and the solemn walls whisper an answer…a long, wild wavering note, high-quavered and keen; and there, riding small and dark at the base of the leaning grandeur, the Navajo man comes singing.

—Maynard Dixon,
The Red Walls of Navajoland

Part of an allure for artists has been the Navajo occupants of Canyon de Chelly. For over two centuries, Navajo have lived in and around the canyon. Early artists perceived the Navajo as an integral part of Canyon de Chelly, timeless partners with the solemn, rock-rimmed landscape. As Navajo rode through the canyons, their high-keyed lilting songs could be heard from far off through the clean air, a slim grace of

Fig. 3
Gray Bartlett, *Abode of the Spirits*, n.d. Oil on canvas,
24 x 30 inches. Trails End Collection, Kalispell, Montana.

Fig. 4
Edgar Payne, *Canyon de Chelly,* ca. 1925.
Oil on canvas, 25 x 30 inches. Arizona West Galleries,
Bill Mc Lemore Photography.

people forever on horseback, it seemed, haughty and proud (figure 4).

Today the Navajo are a viable part of Canyon de Chelly's landscape, still a subject for painters and photographers, but the ubiquitous pickup truck is now the dominant transportation. The Navajo venture into the canyon when spring arrives, to plant—as generations have before—fields of corn, squash, or alfalfa; horses and sheep are turned loose to wander at will; hogans are dusted out, used again; and quiet peaceful days and nights pass. When fall comes, the Navajo leave for their homes up on the rim or down at Chinle. Canyon de Chelly shifts into a quiet period and prepares for the cold winter ahead, a rest for spring and return of the inhabitants.

Paintings, drawings, watercolors, and prints that reflect Canyon de Chelly images have appeared sporadically in exhibit catalogs or in magazine articles, but no comprehensive historical survey of art in these media exists. In contrast, certain photographs of Canyon de Chelly by early photographers such as Timothy O'Sullivan, John K. Hillers, Edward S. Curtis, Ben Wittick, and later visitors such as Laura Gilpin and Ansel Adams, have been reproduced often in scholarly publications, books, or popular magazines. For the latter half of the nineteenth century and into the early twentieth century, photographers were dominant practitioners at Canyon de Chelly, while painters were infrequent visitors. Furthermore, for both painters and photographers, the canyon's visual impact often led them toward similar views, such as of White House Ruin. Together, photographs and paintings reproduced in this book illustrate an important theme for Canyon de Chelly, a disappeared or changed historical, ecological, and geographical past (figure 5).

The images reproduced in the book are only selective fragments drawn from a large array of painters and photographers who have visited the canyon. Some are well known, others less so, and a few of the early ones perhaps not at all. Most paintings and photographs illustrated in the book have never been reproduced before, and are combined with images of Canyon de Chelly by certain artists whose works have appeared consistently in various publications.

In 1938, there was only one permanent custodian at Canyon de Chelly, assisted by two temporary rangers in the summer months. Furthermore, a guide to Southwestern National Monuments published that year left little doubt about the difficult journey into Canyon de Chelly:

> Let no prospective visitor to Canyon de Chelly think he will find a prim little garden spot with graveled walks bordered by mignonette and forget-me-nots. No! Canyon de Chelly is tough. If a visitor bucks his way 95 miles over a none too dependable road, hits the weather right and makes the risky trip up the canyon successfully, he will cherish a never-to-be-forgotten memory. But those who have a distaste for jouncy desert roads, sand in their teeth, and general wear and tear on their constitutions, had better confine their driving to transcontinental highways and leave de Chelly to the Navajo.

Guide to Southwestern Monuments

Even though the road from Ganado to Chinle would not be an all-weather highway until 1959, increased numbers of photographers and painters discovered the pristine beauty and human drama of Canyon de Chelly in the last several decades. Numerous

painting and photography workshops are now held at the canyon each year, particularly during fall when cottonwood leaves turn their golden color. At any time of year, individual artists can be seen behind their cameras or in front of easels.

Tourists started to arrive in greater numbers each year after World War II to the point the canyon now attracts nearly a million visitors a year. Entry in Canyon de Chelly is limited to foot travel, horses, and four-wheel-drive vehicles, and all travelers must secure an authorized Navajo guide or be with a Park ranger. The only exception is the short hike to White House Ruin from White House Overlook.

Thunderbird Lodge in Chinle schedules half-day or full-day trips into Canyon de Chelly and Canyon del Muerto when conditions permit. In addition, numerous overlooks on rims of both canyons afford expansive views.

Whether casual tourist or dedicated artist, all are enthralled with Canyon de Chelly's majestic drama. They leave with vivid memories of an enchanted place, a corrugated landscape where spirits still dwell.

AMONG THE ROCKS, 1849–1900

In August 1849, the United States Army decided to mount a military expedition as retaliation against Navajo raiders for their frequent strikes on New Mexico settlements. Lt. Colonel John M. Washington, military and civil governor of New Mexico, led the campaign, which took over a month and covered nearly 600 miles. James Hervey Simpson, a thirty-six-year-old lieutenant in the Corps of Topographical Engineers, was ordered to accompany the expedition. With Simpson were two assistants, Edward M. Kern, (1823–1863), "topographer and first assistant," and Richard H. Kern (1821–1853), "second assistant and artist." Simpson kept an extensive journal, published as a government document in 1850 and illustrated with lithographs from drawings by Richard Kern, among them the first views of Canyon de Chelly and White House Ruin. Simpson's written description of Canyon de Chelly formed the basis of all successive accounts for nearly thirty years. He provided the first description of Casa Blanca (White House Ruin), and was the first to use the now-current spelling of the name Chelly.

On September 5, 1849, some seventy men, including Colonel Washington, Simpson, and the two Kerns, explored around the head of Canyon del Muerto, probed various side canyons, then traveled a trail along the north rim to near present-day Chinle. Richard Kern sketched the first images of Canyon de Chelly. As his group reached the gorge, Kern made a wash-drawing sketch, *View of the Cañon of Chelly Near Its Head, Five Miles South West of Camp l7, Sept. 5* (figure 6). Another drawing, *Ruins of an Old Pueblo in the Cañon of Chelly, Sept. 8* (figure 7), presents the first view of Canyon de Chelly's most famous ruin, White House Ruin. Kern's drawings of Canyon de Chelly project a rather naïve, simplified directness with little concern for composition, but they are straightforward documents, done in the field with a quick, direct style.

VIEW OF THE CANON OF CHELLY NEAR ITS HEAD,
five miles south west of Camp l7.

Fig. 6

Richard H. Kern, *View of the Cañon of Chelly Near Its Head,* Sept. 5, 1849.
Wash drawing. Library, The Academy of Natural Sciences of Philadelphia.

No. 53.

RUINS OF AN OLD PUEBLO
in the Cañon of Chelly.
Sept 84.

Fig. 7
Richard H. Kern, *Ruins of an Old Pueblo*,
Sept. 8, 1849. Wash drawing. Library, The
Academy of Natural Sciences of Philadelphia.

In 1853, Richard joined the survey party of Captain John W. Gunnison, organized to determine the feasibility of a railroad route from Independence, Missouri, to Salt Lake City. On October 26, 1853, while Gunnison, Kern, and six other members of the survey party were camped in Utah's Sevier Valley, they were attacked and killed by Paiute Indians. Richard Kern died at age thirty-two.

Not until 1859 would another artist document Canyon de Chelly. Joseph Heger (1835–1897), a German-born lithographer, had enlisted in the United States Army in 1855 and served a five-year tour of duty that included action in a punitive expedition directed against the Navajo in 1859. Both Heger's experiences and sketches of that 1859 campaign survive through the diary of John van Duesen DuBois, who served with Heger in Company K of the First Regiment of Mounted Riflemen. In early summer of 1859, DuBois and Heger's regiment undertook an engagement against the Navajo, an expedition that started at Abiquiu, New Mexico, and ended at Canyon de Chelly. On July 20, 1859, DuBois wrote impressions of Canyon de Chelly in his journal:

The descent was truly terrific. We were four hours getting down the 800 feet depth. Mules fell distances of from twenty to forty feet. Two were killed and several saved by their loads which prevented them from striking the rocks in their fall. Looking up it seems as if there was no escape. The stream was running in the cañon, though often, the Indians say its bed is dry. Tall pines look like bushes when contrasted with the sides of this descent. Man and animals on the top, as seen from below, are like mites against the sky. Next to Niagara it is the greatest wonder of Nature I have ever seen. I have a sketch of it which is perfect but can only show half one glance out of a thousand.

We march eleven miles down the cañon—New features and wonders at every turn. Now the cañon narrowed so that its depth appeared doubled and one seemed to be buried in the very center of the earth with a window above large enough for light alone; now the cañon opened—fantastic columns were formed reaching nearly to the top some connected here and there with sides forming gigantic ladders.

—GEORGE HAMMOND, *Campaigns in the West 1856–1861: The Journal and Letters of Colonel John van Duesen DuBois*

Heger made a pencil sketch on paper, Canyon de Chelly in the Navajo Country (figure 8), of the canyon from the rim, probably before he and other soldiers made their descent to the canyon floor. He used a soft, fluid pencil-like technique, perhaps similar to lithographic crayon, suited to quick, spontaneous impressions, useful when involved with the rigors of a military expedition. In 1860, Heger was discharged at Fort Union, New Mexico, and disappeared until 1896, when he surfaced to petition for a military pension. Denied, Heger dropped from sight, never to be heard from again.

A new era in western exploration opened with development and expanded use of portable wet-plate camera equipment and the ability to reproduce photographs for mass distribution. By the late 1860s, those great photographers of the American West—Timothy O'Sullivan, John K. Hillers, William Henry Jackson—had commenced work on various post-Civil War expeditions formed to investigate and report on vast areas of the West as the frontier advanced.

Every major leader—Ferdinand V. Hayden, Clarence King, John Wesley Powell and George M. Wheeler—included photographers in their expeditions. In time, through these photographers' efforts, the West became visually familiar to Americans. The production of photographs with an array of wet-plate camera equipment was difficult. First the camera was placed on a sturdy tripod, then the scene composed and focused in the large camera. In a portable darkroom, usually a small, pyramidal lightproof canvas tent, a light-sensitive coating was made from a chemically treated collodion solution poured over the plate, followed by a quick immersion into a chemical mix for needed light sensitivity. The plate was then inserted into a lighttight holder, attached to the camera, and the exposure made. Each composition took nearly thirty minutes, and the process was repeated for successive photographs. Glass plates had to be developed and fixed in the portable darkroom, so photographs were never candid snapshots. Final prints were the same size as the glass-plate negative since enlargers were not commonly used.

Most early photographers carried several cameras with them, partly in anticipation of accidents and in part to make different-sized negatives. Expeditionary photographers found that the small stereograph camera was practical for photography, and discovered sales of stereographs were a means to increase their income, since almost every large view could be duplicated in the smaller double image.

The first photographs of Canyon de Chelly were made in 1873 by Timothy O'Sullivan (1840–1882). O'Sullivan gained fame as one of the great Civil War photographers, where he learned photography in Matthew Brady's studio under the tutelage of Alexander Gardner. O'Sullivan recorded memorable, haunted aftermaths of battle scenes at places such as Antietam, Gettysburg, Fairfax Court House, Petersburg, and Appomattox, as he followed the Army of the Potomac campaigns through the war years.

Lieutenant George Montague Wheeler formed his first survey party in 1871, under the auspices of the United States Geographical Survey West of the 100th Meridian. O'Sullivan was appointed the expedition photographer. Wheeler's work terminated in 1879 when the Department of the Interior assumed responsibility for all future surveys. The results of Wheeler's surveys appeared in the seven-volume *Report upon United States Geographical Surveys West of the One Hundredth Meridian,* published between 1875 and 1889.

When Wheeler entered the field in 1873, he placed O'Sullivan in charge of a party that departed from Fort Defiance, Arizona, on September 17, 1873, and reached a branch of Canyon de Chelly by the next day. At Canyon de Chelly, O'Sullivan made the first photographs of the canyon. From their camp, "Camp Beauty," established in Monument Canyon at the foot of "Rock People Turned Into," O'Sullivan's group explored the canyon and its prehistoric ruins for seven days. Among his photographs were *Ancient Ruins in Canyon de Chelly, New Mexico, in a Niche Fifty Feet above Present Canyon Bed* (figure 9) and *Ancient Ruins, Cañon de Chelle* (figure 10) (O'Sullivan thought he was still in New Mexico Territory). The figure in the photograph is Alexander Wyant, a well-known eastern landscape painter and a member of the expedition. O'Sullivan's photographs affirm the sacredness of Canyon de Chelly, his response to a place that is unspoiled.

When John K. Hillers (1843–1925) finished his long, productive career as a photographer, he had made over 20,000 negatives for the United States Geological Survey and the Bureau of American Ethnology. Hillers served in the Union Army during the Civil War and at several western garrisons until 1870. By May 1871, Hillers was employed as a teamster in Salt Lake City. There he met John Wesley Powell, who was already a legendary hero after his monumental accomplishment—the 1869 exploration by boat of the Green and Colorado Rivers. Powell returned to Green River, Wyoming, in 1871, with better designed boats and a new crew. Among them was Hillers, listed as boatman. The next year, when Powell's survey arrived at Lee's Ferry in August 1872, Hillers was the expedition photographer.

In July 1879, Hillers returned to New Mexico and Arizona as photographer for Powell's new Bureau of Ethnology. Along with Powell's friend and assistant, James Stevenson, Hillers explored, collected artifacts, and photographed at Zuni, Acoma, the Hopi mesas, and the Rio Grande pueblos, and did initial explorations

Fig. 8
Joseph Heger, *Cañon de Chelly in the Navajo Country,* 1859.
Pencil on paper, 7 x 12¼ inches.
Arizona Historical Society Library.

Fig. 9
Timothy O'Sullivan,
*Ancient Ruins in
Canyon de Chelly,
New Mexico, in a Niche
Fifty Feet above
Present Canyon Bed,*
1873. Photograph.
Collection of the
Center for Creative
Photography.

Fig. 10
Timothy O'Sullivan, *Ancient Ruins, Cañon de Chelle,* 1873. Photograph. National Archives.

among the ruins in Canyon de Chelly. Hillers and Stevenson visited Zuni and the Hopi pueblos in 1881, and from there journeyed northeast to Canyon de Chelly, where Hillers photographed White House Ruin and the canyon's great cliffs.

Intrigued with Canyon de Chelly, Stevenson returned in October 1882 with a large party he assembled at Thomas V. Keam's store at Keams Canyon, Arizona. This was the first expedition aimed at full-scale archaeological research in the canyon. Stevenson's group of nineteen people included his wife, Matilda Coxe Stevenson; two ethnologists, one of them Victor Mindeleff; two teamsters; Colonel H. C. Rizer of the Eureka, Kansas *Herald;* an escort of four soldiers from Fort Wingate; and two photographers, John K. Hillers and Ben Wittick. There were also two Navajo guides, one an important leader, Totsohnii Hastiin (Man of the Big Water Clan), also known as Ganado Mucho. John Lorenzo Hubbell named his famous trading post at Ganado for him.

With his large-format 11 x 14 camera, Hillers photographed Mummy Cave and Antelope House in Canyon del Muerto, Spider Rock, Face Rock, and at Monument Canyon in the main drainage. Among Hiller's photographs from the 1882 expedition is *Captains of the Canyons* (figure 11), a dramatic composition of Spider and Face Rocks in the main canyon. Another photograph, *Canyon de Chelly* (figure 12), demonstrates the expansive upper canyon beyond Spider Rock and Monument Canyon.

George Ben Wittick (1845–1903), the other photographer attached to Stevenson's expedition, had arrived in the Southwest by 1879. Born in Pennsylvania, young Wittick moved with his family to Moline, Illinois. When the Civil War began, he enlisted in a volunteer cavalry regiment stationed at Fort Snelling, Minnesota. Mustered out in 1865, Wittick returned to Moline, and after completion of an apprenticeship with a local photographer, started his own photography business.

In 1878, the Atlantic and Pacific Railroad (later, the Santa Fe) offered Wittick a position as official photographer. He came to Santa Fe in 1879 and, from his gallery, documented the railroad's progress in photographs that started from Albuquerque, New Mexico, ranged westward to Gallup, New Mexico, then followed track construction to Holbrook, Winslow, Flagstaff, Williams, and Kingman, Arizona.

In March 1881, Wittick and a partner opened a second studio in Albuquerque, but this time his major operations were at Gallup and then at Fort Wingate, New Mexico. Wittick probably was at Canyon de Chelly in 1881, since he photographed at Hubbell's Trading Post that year, but his presence at the canyon certainly can be confirmed for 1882. One of his 1882 photographs, *Camp-Cañon de Chelly, Arizona* (figure 13), shows James Stevenson, Matilda Coxe Stevenson, John K. Hillers, and other expedition members, including several Navajo guides, in Stevenson's camp.

Like O'Sullivan and Hillers, Wittick was attracted by the canyon's prehistoric ruins. In *First Ruin, or Forks Ruin* (figure 14), the first significant ruin encountered up from Canyon de Chelly's mouth, Wittick has positioned an expedition member who points to ruins perched high on the cliffs. In another photograph, *Canyon de Chelly* (figure 15), he portrays the immensity of the upper main canyon, where a lone figure

Fig. 11
John K. Hillers, *Captains of the Canyons, Spider Rock,* 1882. Photograph. Flury and Company, Seattle, Washington.

poised against a rock is included to enhance the canyon's great scale. Wittick may have envisioned Canyon de Chelly as the Garden of Eden, a sanctuary of nature; in fact, one of his photographs made during 1882 uses that title. Other Wittick photographs from 1882 include those taken at White House Ruin, Mummy Cave, Face Rock, Monument Canyon, Bear Canyon, Antelope House, Talking Rock, and Spider Rock.

Fig. 12
John K. Hillers, *Canyon De Chelly, Arizona,* 1882. Photograph. Courtesy of the Museum of New Mexico, neg. no. 122772.

Fig. 13 (facing)
Ben Wittick, *Camp Cañon De Chelly,* 1882. Photograph. Courtesy of the School of American Research Collections in the Museum of New Mexico, neg. no. 15475.

When Victor Mindeleff, accompanied by his brother Cosmos, returned to Canyon de Chelly in 1885, Wittick came along as an unofficial photographer. Through the latter half of the 1880s until 1903, Wittick probably made frequent excursions to Canyon de Chelly. Around 1890, for example, he photographed again in the canyon. One of his photographs taken at that time, *Prehistoric Ruins of Canyon de Chelly* (figure 16), indicates his increased ability at composition.

By the late 1880s, photography had undergone profound technical transformation, the cumbersome collodion wet plate being replaced by a dry plate. This

Fig. 14
Ben Wittick, *First Ruin* (or *Forks Ruin*), *Canyon de Chelly, Arizona,* 1882. Photograph. Courtesy of the Museum of New Mexico; neg. no. 15526.

Fig. 15 (facing)
Ben Wittick, *Canyon de Chelly, Arizona,* 1882. Photograph. Courtesy of the School of American Research Collections in the Museum of New Mexico; neg. no. 15464.

innovation, and ones that followed in papers, lenses, and processes, eased the formidable problems confronted by photographers in the field. George Eastman pioneered the way, with roll-holder cameras and bromide-coated paper on which the image could be developed by chemical means rather than printing out in the sun.

As these technical developments unfolded, serious photographers sought new avenues for their expression. They took their cue from painting, their interest in the camera prompted by a wish to use it as an art tool. What was called "pictorial photography" arose, marked by murky, subdued tones driven by impressionistic, soft-focus techniques. Sepia or gold-toned prints, often heavily retouched, even hand-colored images, surfaced from the late 1890s through the second decade of the twentieth century. Many of the photographers who visited Canyon de Chelly in this era were pictorialists, concerned with photography as artistic expression rather than as documentary images.

Fig. 16
Ben Wittick, *Prehistoric Ruins of Canyon de Chelly,* ca. 1890.
Photograph. Courtesy of the School of American Research
Collections in the Museum of New Mexico; neg. no. 15482.

A FAR-OFF PLACE, 1900–1920

As the twentieth century commenced, painters and photographers began to filter slowly into the northeastern Navajo country. Most started the journey to Canyon de Chelly from Gallup, New Mexico, where they had arrived by train—their first destination being John Lorenzo Hubbell's trading post at Ganado, Arizona. Ganado was sixty-five miles northwest of Gallup, a journey that could take two days by horseback, maybe one day with a good buggy team, or four days by freight wagon in good weather. During frigid winter months, the trip might consume nearly ten days. Once at Ganado, artists would outfit for the last thirty miles to Chinle and Canyon de Chelly. Almost all artists who came to Canyon de Chelly agreed it was, indeed, a far-off place.

Perhaps the first artist to stay at Sam Day's post at Chinle, which later became the famous Thunderbird Lodge, was photographer Sumner W. Matteson (1867–1920), who rode into Canyon de Chelly in the summer of 1900 on unique transportation—a bicycle. Matteson was an enthusiastic photographer who traveled more than 25,000 miles and produced over 12,000 photographs as he documented a transitional American West from 1898 to 1908. A freelance photographer, Matteson sold hundreds of his photographs to popular magazines and books as illustrations for some of the best-known travel writers of the time.

Matteson visited the Southwest in 1900, traveling by bicycle from Denver, Colorado, to the Grand Canyon, then on to Acoma and Isleta in New Mexico. En route to Acoma, Matteson visited Canyon de Chelly, where he explored Canyon del Muerto for several days, taking photographs of the impressive cliffs and the Navajo who farmed down in the canyon. Only a small number of landscapes are represented in Matteson's photographs, one of them *Canyon del Muerto* (figure 17). At this time, Matteson used two Kodak folding cameras, the no. 5 cartridge and no. 3 folding pocket camera with roll film, the latter introduced in 1900. His photograph of Canyon del Muerto is a straightforward image with no attempt at pictorial manipulation.

Maynard Dixon (1875–1946) ventured into Canyon de Chelly during the summer of 1902. By the 1940s, Dixon had become one of the West's leading artists, his art being a response to the immense western landscape and the mysticism of Native Americans. In the summer of 1902, Dixon accepted a commission from the Santa Fe Railway and left for the Southwest to join photographer-lecturer Frederick Monsen, who was on his way to photograph Hopi Indians in Arizona. Dixon arrived in Winslow, Arizona, with Monsen, and the two headed north toward the Hopi villages by freight wagon. After exploration in and around Oraibi, Dixon decided to visit John Lorenzo Hubbell's trading post at Ganado in August.

Dixon often ventured over to Sam Day's post at Chinle and from there would explore the coiled recesses of Canyon de Chelly and Canyon del Muerto, impressed with their massive water-stained walls and with the Navajo, wilder than at Ganado. Once Dixon accepted an invitation from photographer Ben Wittick to explore Canyon del Muerto's remote upper reaches. In a letter to Charles F. Lummis, Dixon wrote about difficulties of the trip:

Fig. 17
Sumner W.
Matteson, *Canyon del Muerto,* 1900.
Photograph.
Milwaukee Public
Museum.

Fig. 18
Maynard Dixon, *Canyon del Muerto,* 1902. Pastel on paper, 14½ x 10⅞ inches. Museum of Art, Brigham Young University.

I left here with Ben Wittick a week ago for d. Chelly and got back last evening by the bad lands trail from Chinlee. We made it between noon and sunset and I had a couple of Navajo traveling. I had a fine Indian packing for me. The old boy is still up here and he's a great old braggert. But for me the trip was a failure. When we got out into the Llano de la Larga (named for the water that the Navajo call Pei-k-li-hat-soh) we ran up against a north wind that put me out of business for five days.

—DONALD J. HAGERTY, *Desert Dreams: The Art and Life of Maynard Dixon*

Dixon made several large pastel drawings, among them *Canyon del Muerto* (figure 18), saturated with the canyon's form, color, and drama. Dixon's records indicate that he made other visits to Canyon de Chelly in 1904 and 1905.

In April 1915, Dixon, his wife Lillian, and their five-year-old daughter, Constance, returned to Canyon de

Chelly. Dixon spent several days in the canyon, drawing and painting small oil and watercolor sketches. After his return to San Francisco in late fall, he used one study to paint *Navajo Women Bathing, Canyon de Chelly* (figure 19). Influenced by the impressionist art he had encountered at the 1915 Panama Pacific International Exposition in San Francisco, Dixon experimented with innovative color and high-key palette in the painting. The canvas retains his illustrator's realistic approach to narration, but the color values are pushed to more extremes.

As the twentieth century began, Ben Wittick continued to photograph in Canyon de Chelly. One of his photographs, *Sam E. Day and Four Indians, Sentinel Ruin* (figure 20), documents the activities of Day in 1902, as he and several Navajo assistants probe the floor of Sentinel Ruin in Canyon del Muerto. Among Wittick photographs dated 1903 is one taken in Canyon del Muerto. *Prehistoric Ruins of Cañon de Chelly, Arizona*, also titled *Evening in the Cañon*, (figure 21)

shows Wittick capable of experimentation with his compositions. Mummy Cave, nestled beneath the rock shelter, is a distant centerpiece in the far background, while shadows of a canyon afternoon darken the foreground. A flock of Navajo sheep appears as a white band drawn across the shadow. Here, Wittick has become an artist, the photograph more than just a document.

Thirty-six-year-old Edward S. Curtis (1868–1952) came to Canyon de Chelly in 1904, at the start of a legendary journey to document by photography and words what he thought were vanishing lifeways of the American Indian. Few photographers dedicated themselves to their lifework with as much passion as Curtis. As the twentieth century began, Curtis embarked on an ambitious project to accumulate a comprehensive photographic record of all important North American Indian groups, a mission he would pursue for thirty years. The result, published between 1907 and 1930, was the thirty-volume *North American Indian*.

Fig. 19 (facing) Maynard Dixon, *Navajo Women Bathing, Canyon de Chelly*, 1915. Oil on canvas, 50 x 40 inches. Kennedy Galleries, Inc.

Fig. 20 Ben Wittick, *Sam E. Day and Four Indians, Sentinel Ruin, Canyon del Muerto*, 1902. Photograph. Courtesy of the Museum of New Mexico; neg. no. 109106.

Prehistoric Ruins of Cañon de Chelly Arizona - Evening in the Cañon
Copyright 1903 by Ben Wittick

Fig. 21
Ben Wittick, *Prehistoric Ruins of Cañon de Chelly, Evening in the Cañon,* 1903. Photograph. Courtesy of the Museum of New Mexico; neg. no. 15474.

Curtis encountered Canyon de Chelly in the summer of 1904 while on a trip through Arizona, New Mexico, and southern Colorado. That year Curtis produced one of his greatest photographs, *Canyon de Chelly, Navajo* (figure 22), remarkable for its conveyance of drama. Curtis made no attempt at re-creation of the past nor any presentation of romantic stereotypes. Yet it has spiritual, romantic overtones. Seven Navajo mounted on horses, flanked by a dog, traverse the broad sandy floor of Canyon de Chelly, their figures aligned with the vertical cliffs and level canyon floor. The view is up Canyon de Chelly from just below Wild Cherry Canyon.

However, the one image that supports Curtis's romantic, nostalgic concern for Native Americans was also made at Canyon de Chelly in 1904—*The Vanishing Race* (figure 23). The photograph shows several Navajo riders, dimly illuminated by light on their backs, as they ride down a canyon-floor trail toward dark, barely discernible cliffs, perhaps symbolizing for Curtis an unknowable universe. When he wrote the photograph's caption, his words were metaphors for the theme that inspired his lifework:

> The thought which this picture is meant to convey is that the Indians as a race, already shorn of their tribal strength and stripped of their primitive dress, are passing into the darkness of an unknown future. Feeling that the picture expresses so much of thought that inspired the entire work, (I have) chosen it as the first of the series.
>
> —Edward S. Curtis,
> *The North American Indian*

Curtis printed both *Canyon de Chelly* and *The Vanishing Race* as orotone or gold-tone photographs, besides photogravures, and they became his most popular, definitive images. Gold tone, a luminous gold color with a special iridescence, was obtained by printing a reversed image on a glass plate, then sealing it with a mixture of powdered gold pigment and banana oil. This made such images as *The Vanishing Race* particularly evocative in their nostalgic impressions.

That same year also saw photographer Adam Clark Vroman (1856–1916) at work in Canyon de Chelly. Vroman had spent the first thirty-six years of his life in Illinois. In 1894, he opened a book, stationary, and photo-supply store in Pasadena, California, that soon prospered. A sensitive individual, he possessed a deep appreciation for other cultures, enjoyed intellectual company, collected fine books, and amassed a superb group of Southwestern Indian artifacts.

Charles F. Lummis encouraged Vroman to pursue photography in late 1894, and Vroman's store became one of the first Kodak outlets in Los Angeles. Between 1897 and 1904, Vroman made trips to the pueblos of Arizona and New Mexico, where he photographed Pueblo and Navajo groups. The last trip to the Southwest was made in 1904, and this time Vroman included Canyon de Chelly in his itinerary. Vroman made a number of fine photographs in the canyon, among them *White House Ruin* (figure 24). Other subjects for his camera included Mummy Cave, Antelope House, and the magnificent cliffs. He rarely enlarged his photographs but produced crisp, meticulous contact prints on standard chloride paper. In spite of his role as a dealer of Kodak roll-film cameras, he preferred to use the more cumbersome large-view camera with dry plates, from which he developed and printed his photographs. Like many other serious amateurs, Vroman never exhibited his work and considered his photographs extensions of personal pleasure.

Charles Fletcher Lummis (1859–1928) explored Canyon de Chelly in 1906 and may have been there earlier. In 1895, Lummis had assumed editorship of *The Land of Sunshine* (later, *Out West*), a magazine that promoted the beauty of Southern California, and under his energetic direction, circulation rapidly increased as the result of a new literary and cultural identity.

Lummis visited John Lorenzo Hubbell at Ganado in May and June of 1906 and, while headquartered there, toured Canyon de Chelly. On the trip with Lummis were Bertha Page, a daughter born out of wedlock in 1879, and his secretary, Gertrude Reidt, who became Lummis's third wife in 1915. By the early 1900s, Lummis was a skilled, prolific photographer. The photographic traditions of portraiture, landscape, and photojournalism had emerged by the start of the twentieth century, and Lummis participated in all of them.

His confirmation as a photographer began in the mid-1880s, instilled by interest to use photographs as visual supplements to his prolific writings and to advance various causes. Lummis preferred the dry-plate photo process with its wider range of shutter speeds that permitted significantly better action shots. He printed his own work with two photographic processes—the cyanotype and the salted-paper print. Invented in the 1840s, the cyanotype

(from Greek words meaning "dark blue impression,") was, as words indicate, a blueprint photograph.

When Lummis took the photograph *Antelope House Ruins* (figure 25), he used the cyanotype process. The bright sun at Canyon de Chelly was an effective light source for cyanotype prints because the chemicals utilized are sensitive to ultraviolet rays in sunlight. The cyanotype was the fastest, most simple, least expensive photographic technique, and Lummis favored the process over others. His foremost concern was for the record of a place, person, or event, with art being only a secondary concern in his photography.

Born in Corvallis, Oregon, Louis B. Akin (1868–1913), grew up around the mountains of Oregon. In 1898, after employment as a sign painter in Portland for several years, Akin arrived in New York to study at William Merritt Chase's New York art school. In 1903, the Santa Fe Railway offered Akin a commission to paint Hopi Indians for one of the railroad's advertising campaigns. Akin arrived in northern Arizona in September 1903 and proceeded on to Oraibi. During a year-long stay, Akin completed nearly

Fig. 22
Edward S. Curtis, *Canyon de Chelly, Navajo*, 1904. Gold-tone photograph. Flury and Company, Seattle, Washington.

thirty canvases, and one, *In Oraibi Plaza*, was exhibited and illustrated in the 1905 catalog of the National Academy of Design's Annual Exhibition. Afterwards, Akin returned to New York for a year, then came back to the Southwest in 1906, settling in Flagstaff, Arizona.

Sometime in 1908, Akin ventured into Canyon de Chelly as part of an extensive trip he made eastward from the Hopi mesas. He began at Oraibi, then moved over to Second Mesa to meet photographer Frederick Monsen, then rode through Keams Canyon to Ganado, and from there went to Canyon de Chelly. Once there, Akin spent ten days sketching and painting among the sheltering walls and prehistoric ruins. Several paintings survive; one of them, *Spider Rock* (figure 26), was presented to Hubbell. Akin returned to Canyon de Chelly in November 1912, where he worked on preliminary studies for a mural commission destined for the American Museum of Natural History's new room of Southwest Cultures. However, he contracted pneumonia and died at Flagstaff in January 1913.

Frederick I. Monsen (1865–1929), a San Francisco photographer, made landscape and figure studies in Canyon del Muerto and Canyon de Chelly as early as 1899. While still a young man, Monsen accepted photograph projects that took him throughout the West, some of which included assignments from William Henry Jackson. By 1893, he had started to construct a lecture series based on his explorations and photography, although he continued to accompany other expeditions. From 1895 to 1899, Monsen traveled throughout the Southwest, particularly in Hopi and Navajo country, sometimes with friends Adam Clark Vroman and Arnold Genthe. By 1900, Monsen had established a studio in San Francisco, where he created enlargements of his photographs. He and his sons hand colored lantern slides, which Monsen called

colorgraphs, further enhancing his reputation.

In 1908, Monsen returned to Canyon de Chelly, this time accompanied by George Eastman. The result was a small pamphlet, *With a Kodak in the Land of the Navajo*, written by Monsen apparently at Eastman's request and published by Eastman Kodak in 1909. Four black-and-white photographs reproduced in the publication portray places in Canyon de Chelly or Canyon del Muerto. Among Monsen's photographs from the 1908 trip is *Spider Rock* (figure 27). Monsen used his Kodak camera as an artistic device, his prints being carefully composed with a perceptive eye. The photograph of Spider Rock is a dramatic image with pictorialist overtones. A Navajo has paused before the great monolith, his figure and horse in perfect alignment with the vertical shaft of Spider Rock.

Francis J. McComas (1875–1938) left Australia in 1898 to study art in San Francisco, where he worked under Arthur F. Mathews at the California School of Design until 1900, when he departed to study in France. After McComas returned to San Francisco in 1902 from the Academie Julian in Paris, he became nationally known for his watercolor paintings expressed in the warm monochrome of decorative tonalism. During the fall and winter of 1909–1910, he explored Hopi villages and Canyon de Chelly, then investigated Acoma and Zuni in New Mexico. A medium best suited to his vision, McComas's ability with water-color, as in *The White House, Canyon de Chelly* (figure 28), reflects a mature style that uses flattened shapes and flowing compositions. By 1913, he had acquired a formidable reputation and numerous prizes, which culminated in an invitation to exhibit at the International Exhibition of Modern Art held at New York's Sixty-Ninth Regiment Armory.

Between 1907 and 1924, Ferdinand Burgdorff

Fig. 23
Edward S. Curtis, *The Vanishing Race,* 1904. Gold-tone
photograph. Collection of Donald J. Hagerty.

Fig. 24
Adam C. Vroman, *White House Ruin,* 1904. Photograph.
Collection of the Center for Creative Photography.

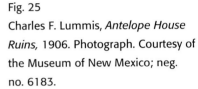

Fig. 25
Charles F. Lummis, *Antelope House Ruins,* 1906. Photograph. Courtesy of the Museum of New Mexico; neg. no. 6183.

(1881–1975) made numerous trips to the Southwest from his home on California's Monterey Peninsula. Even after 1924, Burgdorff would undertake periodic excursions into Arizona, sometimes accompanied by other artist friends such as James Swinnerton. Born in Cleveland, Ohio, Burgdorff studied at the Cleveland School of Art and in Paris with Rene Menard and Florence Este. In 1907, inspired by western landscape painters, Burgdorff worked in Santa Fe, New Mexico, for a period, then moved to Carmel, California. On trips to the Southwest, Burgdorff painted at the Grand Canyon,

Fig. 26
Louis B. Akin,
Spider Rock,
1908. Oil on
canvas, 16 x 12
inches. National
Park Service,
Hubbell Trading
Post National
Historic Site.
Photograph by
Lisa E. Wallace.

Fig. 27
Frederick I. Monsen,
Spider Rock, 1908.
Photograph. National
Park Service, Hubbell
Trading Post National
Historic Site. Photograph
by Lisa E. Wallace.

Fig. 28
Francis J. McComas, *The White House, Canyon de Chelly,* 1909. Watercolor, 22½ x 28½ inches.
George Stern Fine Arts.

Zuni, Acoma, and other Pueblo communities, and on the sprawling Navajo Reservation. In 1910, Burgdorff visited Canyon de Chelly, where he painted *Casa Blanca, Canyon de Chelly* (figure 29).

An art critic once declared that Burgdorff's aim in painting was not to attract attention by spectacular compositions but to use reasonable techniques so the public would not sense the method, only the subject. Burgdorff's painting of White House Ruin fits within the tenets of realism, yet manages to convey a romantic interpretation of the canyon's mystery and drama.

When William R. Leigh (1866–1955) contacted William H. Simpson, the Santa Fe Railway's advertising manager, in 1906 with a proposal to furnish a painting of the Grand Canyon in exchange for free passage from New York City, he was prompted by a consummate desire to paint western subjects. An accomplished, technically proficient painter by 1900, Leigh received his first art instruction at age fourteen from the Maryland Institute in Baltimore. From 1883 through 1895, he studied abroad, primarily at the prestigious Royal Academy in Munich, Germany. Leigh returned to the United States in 1896 and opened a studio in New York City, where he worked as an illustrator for *Scribner's Magazine* and *Collier's,* painting portraits and landscapes between magazine commissions.

In April 1912, John Lorenzo Hubbell received a letter from artist Albert Groll, introducing "William R. Leigh, an old friend of mine and a fine artist." Hubbell invited Leigh to Ganado. Leigh arrived at the post in early summer and began painting numerous sketches of the landscape and Navajo subjects. Three weeks later, two young artists, Emry Kopta and Alonzo Megargee, rode into the trading post. After some discussion, the three artists decided they would visit Canyon de Chelly. For ten days in July 1912, Leigh, Kopta, and Megargee explored the canyon, climbed into prehistoric ruins, camped near springs, and sketched the canyon's landscapes. Leigh painted numerous oil sketches while in Canyon de Chelly that year. The Gilcrease Museum has several of these studies, including *Sunset, Canyon de Chelly* (figure 30). These small works are full of the canyon's color and mood, prompted by Leigh's responsiveness to the artistic challenge posed by the landscape.

Fig. 29
Ferdinand Burgdorff, *Casa Blanca, Canyon de Chelly*, 1910. Oil on board, 18 x 24 inches. Collection of Arizona West Galleries, Scottsdale, Arizona.

Photographer Roland Reed (1864–1934) visited Canyon de Chelly in 1913. From 1908 until his death in 1934, Reed photographed the Hopi, Navajo, Blackfeet, Flathead, Piegan, Chippewa, Cheyenne, and other groups. His photograph *The Pottery Maker* won a gold medal at the 1915 Panama Pacific International Exposition in San Francisco. Reed's photograph *Alone with the Past* (figure 31), which shows two blanketed Indians posed across the wash from White House Ruin, is an example of his pictorialist style. As a pictorialist, Reed concentrated on specific techniques, dramatic close-ups and composition, soft-focus lenses, and other manipulations to produce images he considered art. He usually portrayed Native Americans as proud, primitive people from an earlier era. Reed took meticulous care in the creation of his images and never sanctioned their use for commercial purposes. Harmony is an integral part of his photography, as in *Alone with the Past,* where he has invoked a mood of reverence for an ancient, lost world. Like most pictorialists, Reed adopted printing techniques from other media and mixed or manipulated his prints to convert photographs into handcrafted art.

Fig. 30
William R. Leigh, *Sunset, Canyon de Chelly,* 1912. Oil on board, 13⅛ x 16¾ inches. Gilcrease Museum, Tulsa.

Two artists whose names loom large in Canyon de Chelly history are Edgar Payne and Carl Oscar Borg. Edgar A. Payne (1883–1947) grew up in Missouri's Ozark Mountains and left home at fourteen to pursue a painting career. By 1907, he had landed in Chicago, where he enrolled in classes at the Art Institute of Chicago, only to drop out within two weeks to pursue painting through his own self-education.

Payne sought out isolated environments that allowed him solitude for his work, first visiting the Southwest in 1916 at the invitation of William H. Simpson. Accompanied by his wife, Elsie Palmer Payne, also an artist, Payne arrived in Gallup, New Mexico, on June 25, 1916. Roman Hubbell, son of Lorenzo Hubbell, met him there and arranged for special automobile transportation to Canyon de Chelly. The Paynes stayed four months in the area, with almost daily trips into the canyon by wagon. From the first moment he viewed the canyon, Payne was enthralled with Canyon de Chelly's beauty and Navajo lifeways.

From small oil sketches made on his explorations through the canyon during 1916, Payne painted several large canvases, including *Sunset, Canyon de Chelly*

Fig. 31
Roland Reed,
*Alone with the
Past,* 1913.
Photograph.
Kramer
Gallery, Inc.
Minneapolis,
Minnesota.

EDGAR PAYNE

(figure 32). The painting portrays red-orange sand-stone walls, that enclose a group of Navajo riders on the canyon floor. The walls are painted in a solid, monumental way with light manipulated to reinforce landscape forms. *Canyon de Chelly* (figure 33), in the collections at Hubbell Trading Post National Historic Site, appears to be an early Payne, probably from 1916. This painting is different from his later canyon works,

Fig. 32
Edgar Payne, *Sunset, Canyon de Chelly,* 1916. Oil on canvas, 26 x 32 inches. Redfern Gallery.

with a close-up view of Navajo horsemen next to a dark, shadowed wall, their figures and the canyon floor bathed by an intense white light and near vaporization from the bright sun.

The other artist whose name is synonymous with Canyon de Chelly is Carl Oscar Borg (1879–1947). Born in Dals-Grinstad, Sweden, Borg's formal education ended in 1893, when he started an apprenticeship as a house painter and decorator in Vanesborg. By 1899, Borg had moved to Stockholm, then went to England in 1900, where he painted portrait and marine subjects in addition to theater sets for the Drury Lane Theater. In exchange for free passage to America in 1901, Borg painted pictures for the captain of a transatlantic vessel, then disembarked at Norfolk, Virginia. After several jobs in New York and Philadelphia, Borg was hired in 1903 as an able-bodied seaman on a ship destined for California. When the ship reached San Francisco, Borg left for Los Angeles, where he decided to settle. By 1909, Borg was proficient in oil, watercolor, monotype, gouache, pen, and pencil mediums.

Borg received a commission in 1916 from the Bureau of American Ethnology and the University of California to document Hopi and Navajo Indians. From June to September 1916, he explored and painted at Walpi, the Grand Canyon, and Canyon de Chelly. From this experience he determined that Native Americans and the Southwest landscapes would be his principal subjects.

Fig. 33
Edgar Payne, *Canyon de Chelly,* 1916. Oil on canvas, 27½ x 33¾. National Park Service, Hubbell Trading Post National Historic Site. Photograph by Lisa E. Wallace.

Fig. 34
Carl Oscar Borg,
Sunset, Canyon de Chelly, 1916. Oil on canvas, 40 x 30 inches. Santa Fe Railway Collection of Southwestern Art.

One of Borg's paintings done at Canyon de Chelly in 1916, *Sunset, Canyon de Chelly* (figure 34), reverberates with the canyon's light and color. The red sandstone walls are bathed with late afternoon light, shadows highlighted in crevices and on the canyon floor. Like most early artists at Canyon de Chelly, Borg included Navajo figures in the painting, his response to the relationship between the Navajo and their canyon environment. Enthralled with Canyon de Chelly's palpable sense of a long human past, Borg returned in 1917 and 1918. In his notebook of poems for 1918, Borg, a consummate romantic, wrote "The White House":

> When the sun glides down to his gorgeous haven, behind the crest of the canyon's rim, and shadows enshroud the world. We, strangers of alien blood and race, dream before your silent walls. Tis then we bridge the ages and stand before the things that were.
>
> Monument, older than the memories of kings! Do you, like ourselves, grow sad thinking of your forgotten past? Your white towers gleam like sacred flames in the canyon's shadowy night. And your builders, lost in the days that have passed, seem to gather beneath your crumbling ruins: Chiefs with solemn faces; Mothers of Clans now lost; Priests with rain-cloud masks on their heads; dancers and singers; old age and youth…across the crowded centuries you come.
>
> Lost loves and hates…children's faces with dimpling smiles…you come and go in the spell woven by evening dusk…and you fade like ghosts in the morning light.

> And nothing is left but the crumbling walls of a City of Ages Past.

> —Carl Oscar Borg, 1918

Among the most skilled wood-block printers and etchers of his time, Borg made a drypoint etching, *White House* (figure 35), a work which connects the poem and his spiritual, mystical feel for time.

Eastern landscape artist C. Bertram Hartman (1882–1960) wandered through Canyon de Chelly in 1916, and returned in 1917. He was born in Junction City, Kansas, and studied at the Art Institute of Chicago, Royal Academy in Munich, Germany, and in Paris. Hartman exhibited at San Francisco's Panama Pacific International Exposition in 1915 and again in the Post-Exposition held there a year later. Three of Hartman's Canyon de Chelly paintings are in the collections at Hubbell Trading Post National Historic Site. One painting is *Talking Rock, Canyon de Chelly* (figure 36). Another canvas, with a date of 1917, is titled *Spider Rock and Rainbow* (figure 37) and inscribed for "J. L. Hubbell." These paintings suggest that Hartman was an early modernist painter, influenced by the Fauvists. They are infused with bright color, rely upon some form of distortion, such as the figures of Navajo riders, and are strident with personal emotionalism.

Herbert F. Robinson (1865–1956), an engineer and amateur photographer, arrived in New Mexico in 1902. Born in Illinois, Robinson moved to Phoenix, Arizona, with his family in 1887. He grew up there, and by 1898 had been appointed adjutant general of Arizona Territory. Four years later he moved to Albuquerque, New Mexico, when he received a position as an irrigation engineer for the United States Indian Bureau.

Fig. 35
Carl Oscar Borg, *The White House,* ca. 1918–20.
Drypoint etching, 15¾ x 11⅜ inches. Santa Barbara
Museum of Art.

Fig. 36
C. Bertram Hartman, *Talking Rock, Canyon de Chelly*, 1916. Oil on board, $16^{15}/_{16}$ x $11^{15}/_{16}$ inches. National Park Service, Hubbell Trading Post National Historic Site. Photograph by Lisa E. Wallace.

Robinson's photograph, *White House Ruins* (figure 38), was taken about 1919, when he explored the Canyon de Chelly area. His photographs have no artistic pretensions but seem more documentary in nature. Never a proficient technician, Robinson sent his negatives to a commercial studio in Albuquerque for development of prints. His work reflects that of an ardent amateur who worked at photography for over twenty years. The Robinson collection of 1,000 negatives held by the Museum of New Mexico is largely composed of views that depict Native American life in the Southwest.

Fig. 37 (facing)
C. Bertram Hartman, *Spider Rock and Rainbow, Canyon de Chelly,* 1917. Oil on canvas, 20 x 24 inches. National Park Service, Hubbell Trading Post National Historic Site. Photograph by Lisa E. Wallace.

Fig. 38
Herbert F. Robinson, *White House Ruins, Canyon de Chelly, Arizona,* 1919. Photograph. Courtesy of the Museum of New Mexico; neg. no. 37161.

TIME AND CULTURE, 1920–1945

From the 1920s to the early 1940s, painters and photographers who encountered Canyon de Chelly were artists whose work represented both a commitment to American subject matter and intense personal reservations about American urban growth and commercial exploitation. They made their homes in places such as Gallup, Taos, or Santa Fe in New Mexico, or San Francisco, Los Angeles, Laguna Beach, Santa Barbara, and Palm Springs in California. Most felt spiritually rejuvenated from the eternal landscapes of Canyon de Chelly, their art—in particular, painting—concerned with an unreserved, enthusiastic response drawn from the canyon's dramatic beauty and exotic quality of Navajo life. With few exceptions, artists who worked at Canyon de Chelly between 1920 and 1945 were romantic realists, enthused by their need to search for a wilderness of untamed nature, where time and culture were suspended.

Among numerous artists attracted to the Southwest after the First World War was Joseph R. Willis (1876–?), an art student when the Spanish-American War began in 1898, and his first job was as a war-story illustrator for the *Atlanta Constitution*. From 1902 to 1903, he studied art at the Art Students League in New York under Robert Henri, and then, in a radical shift, appeared in vaudeville productions throughout the United States. Attracted by the energy of motion-picture cartoons, Willis eventually secured a position as an animation illustrator in Hollywood just before World War I.

In 1917, Willis moved to New Mexico, where he opened a photography studio at Gallup, followed by another in Albuquerque in the early 1930s. He spent summers on reservations in New Mexico and Arizona painting Indian life. While Willis was a competent painter, his photograph *Navajo Men and Horses, White House Ruin* (figure 39) illustrates that he had a fine grasp of creation and drama in photography. Both artistic statement and historical document, the photograph portrays three Navajo stopped before White House Ruin, while their horses graze nearby. The way Willis framed men and horses points the viewer toward the distant ruin. The photograph captured the vegetation pattern and stream configuration in front of the ruin, a pattern and view that have changed.

Through the 1920s and until 1932, Carl Oscar Borg made annual pilgrimages to Canyon de Chelly. He celebrated the canyon's landscapes and peoples in drawings, watercolor, drypoint etching, woodblock prints, gouache, and oil. Almost without exception, Borg connected Canyon de Chelly's landscapes with Navajo culture; thus a recurrent theme in his images is a group of serene, dignified Navajo on horseback, flanked by red sandstone cliffs as they ride across the canyon floor.

In the canyon Borg made studies, generally small gouache or watercolor sketches, along with pencil drawings. Upon his return to the studio, he painted larger canvases, the field sketches acting as inspiration for composition and color. Borg often expanded his broad brush strokes in studio paintings to enhance light and shadow interplay on the canyon walls.

Fig. 39
Joseph R. Willis, *Navajo Men and Horses, White House Ruins*, ca. 1920. Photograph. Courtesy of the Museum of New Mexico; neg. no. 90508.

Fig. 40
Carl Oscar Borg, *Canyon de Chelly at Night,* 1920s.
Oil on canvas, 25 x 30 inches. Arlington Gallery.

Paintings such as *Canyon de Chelly* (see figure 2) evoke that mystic romanticism prevalent in his work. Never reluctant to experiment, and inspired by the canyon's different moods, he painted *Canyon de Chelly at Night* (figure 40), a canvas that has the quality of night rather than physical specifics of a precise location.

Carl Oscar Borg had a symbolic relationship with Hopi and Navajo country, a land he often referred to as the Province of Tusayan. Borg wrote an essay for *Touring Topics* in 1929 that included a number of his Canyon de Chelly pencil drawings illustrated in rotogravure and expressed his thoughts:

> Although everything is peaceful, silent and impressive, one can still feel and see the struggles that have taken place here. The lonely mesas, with saw-tooth backs like strange monsters rising from the plains, the boulder-strewn hillsides, skylines broken in a thousand strange forms, the primeval struggles that have made this land, are visible everywhere. But now is peace and quiet and it seems difficult and unreal to think of the crowded cities that lie beyond these wide and distant horizons.

> In its varying moods this country seems endless. There is no end to the light, color, form and distances. Everything is enveloped in a haze—blue, yellow, pink and lilac. And the night! How wonderful, how mysterious and magnificent! How unlike anything most men ever see—silent, fathomless, shadowy—the stars like jewels against the black curtain of the sky.

> By day or night this old land is always calm and majestic. The ruins that are scattered over it are also a never-ending wonder. On the big mesas, on the windswept plains, are these abandoned ruins of cities of the long ago. All this that man has forgotten, Nature seems to cherish. These strange, spectral, gleaming ruins of palaces and cities in the caves of Canyon de Chelly, Canyon del Muerto, and others all add to the mystery. All of them form questions on our lips. But the answer is hidden in the sphinxlike silence of the desert.

> And so, for those that love the primitive beauty of simplicity, this land of enchantment and the inhabitants that dwell under its blazing skies will furnish inspiration of the sublimest nature, and a visit to the land of Tusayan should prove a never-to-be-forgotten experience.

> —Carl Oscar Borg,
> *The Province of Tusayan*

Not all of Borg's work was done within the canyon itself, for in *Navajo Land* (figure 41) he depicts the mouth of Canyon de Chelly as it trails into Chinle Wash. The canvas is saturated with the bright light of open desert, while the landscape seems to coil around the wash as it moves toward the horizon.

Like Carl Oscar Borg, Edgar Payne chose Canyon de Chelly as a main theme in his paintings during the 1920s and 1930s. Stark cliffs and Navajo inhabitants

were recurrent subjects for Payne's bold, structured, Postimpressionistic work. While camped in the canyon, Payne made numerous small oil sketches of canyon formations, visual facts that captured structure and color. Paintings such as *Canyon de Chelly* (figure 42) were done with quick, broad brush strokes—memories for large studio paintings; however, they also served for learning. Payne made numerous pencil or charcoal sketches, such as *Canyon de Chelly* (figure 43), an attentive study that elaborated basic structure and explored the soul of what he wished to visualize.

Payne created monumental canvases of Canyon de Chelly. Above all, he believed, an artist must respond to an unpolluted natural world in order to sense the spiritual flow that encircles animate and inanimate forms. In his paintings *Canyon de Chelly* (figure 44) and *Canyon de Chelly* (figure 45), Payne has created large rock masses on the canvases, almost architectonic in execution, marked with visual harmony through organized form, color, and light. For Payne, light reinforced forms; however, he countered the brilliant, intense light reflected from Canyon de Chelly's walls with balanced dark-and-light arrangement patterns. This is evident in *Blue Canyon* (see frontispiece), in which he approached a view of Canyon de Chelly not from the canyon floor but from the rim, to paint an image that uses bands of color—light as color—a soliloquy on the act of light.

The visual relationship between landscape and Navajo is a constant theme in Payne's Canyon de Chelly work. Like other painters who visited the canyon, Payne sensed that the Navajo were an integral part of the landscape. With few exceptions, Payne included Navajo figures in paintings such as *Navajo Stronghold* (figure 46) and *Canyon de Chelly* (see figure 4), their presence an essential part of a rock-rimmed, red-earth paradise.

During the late summer of 1923, Maynard Dixon again returned to Arizona. For nearly four months, he sketched and painted aspects of Hopi culture at Walpi. In early November 1923, Dixon and Emry Kopta, also in residence at Walpi, took a long, cold wagon ride to Chinle and into the vastness of Canyon del Muerto. Later, in his San Francisco studio, he painted *Canyon del Muerto* (figure 47 on page 69), a painting that reflected his new realism—broad, uncomplicated but with strong color areas and simplification of essential forms.

Fig. 41
Carl Oscar Borg, *Navajo Land,* ca. 1922–28. Oil on canvas, 30 x 40 inches.
Collection of Arizona West Galleries.

Fig. 42 (facing)
Edgar Payne, *Canyon de Chelly,* 1925. Oil on board,
11¼ x 9¼ inches. Goldfield Galleries.

Fig. 43
Edgar Payne, *Canyon de Chelly,* ca. 1925. Charcoal on paper,
16 x 18 inches. Collection of Mr. & Mrs. Martin Medak.

Another California artist, Hansen Duvall Puthuff (1875–1972), sometimes accompanied Edgar Payne to Canyon de Chelly. Born in Missouri, Puthuff moved with his foster mother to Colorado in 1889, where he studied at the University of Denver Art School. In 1903, he arrived in Los Angeles and for the next twenty-three years worked as a commercial artist, primarily as a painter of billboards; but whenever possible, he painted land-scapes. In 1926, Puthuff turned from commercial art to pursue easel painting and exhibitions. An important figure in Southern California art, his paintings won numerous awards at exhibitions.

Like many California artists in the 1920s and 1930s, Puthuff was attracted to the brilliant color, light, and open space of Navajo country. He preferred to paint plein air, and his paintings have that warm vitality and fluent interpretive style based on direct

Fig. 44 (facing)
Edgar Payne, *Canyon de Chelly,* 1920s. Oil on canvas,
28 x 34 inches. Fleischer Museum.

Fig. 45
Edgar Payne, *Canyon de Chelly,* 1920s. Oil on canvas,
28 x 34 inches. Springville Museum of Art.

observation of nature. His painting *Canyon de Chelly* (figure 48) expresses a tonal quality, subtle harmonious hues, and dynamic design that enhance massive canyon walls towering over a Navajo camp at their base.

Gordon Coutts (1868–1937) was probably at Canyon de Chelly around 1929, where he painted *Canyon de Chelly* (figure 49). Coutts, born in Glasgow, Scotland, studied art there, in London, and then at the Academie Julian in Paris. In the early 1890s, he moved to Melbourne, Australia, then returned to London in 1899, where he exhibited at the prestigious Royal Academy. In 1902, Coutts relocated to San Francisco and soon was an active member and exhibitor at the Bohemian Club. He was awarded a medal at the Alaska-Yukon-Pacific Exposition at Seattle in 1909.

Bronchial problems led him to Tangiers, Morocco, and finally to Palm Springs, California, in 1925, where he settled permanently. He continued his trips through Arizona and New Mexico and into Mexico, painting the region's landscapes and people. His painting of Canyon de Chelly features no recognizable geographical location; instead Coutts interprets from a romantic vision to reform the canyon landscape, his Navajo riders illuminated with light and dark contrasts through the use of broken brush strokes reminiscent of the French Impressionists.

Raymond Jonson (1891–1982), alone among all the painters attracted to Canyon de Chelly, translated his observations into abstract, formal images, an artistic

Fig. 46
Edgar Payne, *Navajo Stronghold,* ca. 1925. Oil on canvas, 28 x 34 inches. Collection of Mr. & Mrs. Gerald Waldman.

Fig. 47
Maynard Dixon, *Canyon del Muerto,* 1923. Oil on canvas, 30 x 25 inches. Redfern Gallery.

Fig. 48
Hansen D. Puthuff, *Canyon de Chelly,* 1925. Oil on canvas,
30 x 25 inches. Private collection.

language that stressed color and pure form. Jonson acquired his early art education at the Portland, Oregon Museum Art School. After one year, he left for Chicago, where he enrolled at the Chicago Academy of Arts and supplemented with night classes at the Art Institute of Chicago. A poet friend, John Curtis Underwood, invited Jonson to New Mexico in the summer of 1922. Three years later, Jonson made Santa Fe his permanent residence. There he started to paint abbreviated, stylized landscape work known as the *Earth Rhythms* series. They were marked by an increasingly semiabstract form as Jonson struggled to discover basic rhythms in his compositions.

In search of inspirational landscapes, Jonson visited the Grand Canyon in 1927. During that year he stopped at Canyon de Chelly, with the result, *Cañon de Chelly* (figure 50), painted in 1928. In this canvas, nature was still there but primarily as a source of shapes and their relationships. Furthermore he felt that reality's essence, rather than its descriptive qualities, should emerge from the painting surface. The painting's rhythms, colors, and textures are meant to be equals of the rhythm, color, and textures of the painter's sensations.

No discussion of Canyon de Chelly's artists would be complete without Everett Ruess (1914–1934). Ruess explored the California and Southwest deserts on foot, his companions only a burro or horse, starting in the summer of 1930 when he was sixteen. Even at that age, Ruess had abundant boldness in his inspirational search for beauty and adventure, and eventually built this determined obsession into a unique quest. In the spring of 1931, he decided to explore northeastern Arizona. Alone, virtually penniless, Ruess tramped across California and Arizona to Kayenta, where he stopped at John Wetherill's trading post. In early May, Ruess arrived at Chinle after a four-day, eighty-mile trip from Kayenta. For twelve days, he explored silent places in Canyon de Chelly and Canyon del Muerto, documenting his impressions in pencil and watercolor sketches. Sometimes he sold these and other sketches for supply money.

Ruess returned to Canyon de Chelly in July 1932, making a deserted Navajo hogan his campsite. In a journal entry, Ruess recalled his experience:

I passed the last Navajo encampments and stopped for a space in a deserted hogan, constructed of clean-limbed cottonwood, with singing water at the door and sighing leaves overhead—tall, gracefully arched trees screening the sky with a glistening pattern of dappled green, and above and beyond the gorgeous vermilion cliffs. All day I would brood in the cool of the hogan, lying on the diamond saddle blanket I bought from old Dilatsi. Beneath it was a swirl of crisp brown leaves, over the earth floor. Now and then a trickle of sand pouring through a crack in the roof would sift down, rustling the leaves, and the circle of sunshine from the skylight would move from hour to hour. At evening, I would go out into the glade and climb high above the river to the base of the cliff. I would gather scarlet flowers and come down when the stars gleamed softly. Sighing winds would eddy down the canyon, swaying the tree tops. Then the

Fig. 49
Gordon Coutts, *Canyon de Chelly,* ca. 1929. Oil on canvas,
22¼ x 28¼ inches. Collection of Mr. & Mrs. M. E. Burkholder,
Scottsdale, Arizona.

Fig. 50
Raymond Jonson,
Cañon de Chelly,
ca. 1928. Oil and sand
on canvas, 54¼ x 38
inches. Phoenix Art
Museum; museum
purchase with funds
provided by an
anonymous donor.

Fig. 51
Everett Ruess, *Canyon del Muerto,* 1932–33. Wood-block print, 10 x 12 inches. Private collection.

leaves would cease to tremble; only the sound of rippling water would continue, and the spirit of peace and somnolence would pervade the grove, as the red embers of my fire one by one turned black, and shadows deepened into a gently surging slumber.

—On Desert Trails with Everett Ruess

The young artist's final journey to Canyon de Chelly came in May 1934. With some insight into his own destiny, perhaps, Ruess mused about life in a letter to his brother while camped alone in the canyon:

Strange sad winds sweep down the canyon, roaring in the firs and the tall pines, swaying their crests. I don't know how you feel about it, Edward, but I can never accept life as a matter of course. Much as I seem to have shaped my own way, following after my own thinking and my own desires, I never cease to wonder at

the impossibility that I live. Even when to my senses the world is not incredibly beautiful or fantastic, I am overwhelmed by the appalling strangeness and intricacy of the curiously tangled knot of life, and at the way that knot unwinds, making everything clear and inevitable, however unfortunate or wonderful.

—On Desert Trails with Everett Ruess

Later that year, twenty-year-old Ruess left Escalante, Utah, in November, headed into the trackless wilderness of the Kaiparowits Plateau. In early February 1935, Ruess's parents, alarmed at the lack of correspondence from their son, alerted authorities in Escalante. A search party was formed, but they found only Ruess's two burros in Davis Gulch, a side canyon near the Escalante River's confluence with the Colorado River. Sometime in March 1935, searchers discovered Ruess's bootprints on the rim of Hole-in-the-Rock. And that was the end of it; no trace thereafter—just endless speculation over the years on Ruess as myths about his life emerged.

Ruess's writings survive his short, energetic life, with the exception of his 1934 journal, along with some art. Among drawings, watercolors, and prints are several linoleum block prints, including *Canyon del Muerto* (figure 51). It is a simple, balanced image that reflects Ruess's search for underlying truth and testaments about his love for remote places such as Canyon de Chelly.

The year 1937 saw the final visit of William R. Leigh to Canyon de Chelly. This time he was joined by his wife, Ethel Traphagen, a New York artist and fashion designer. Together they established the Traphagen School of Design in New York, where Leigh instructed students in drawing and painting. From his artifact-crammed studio at West 57th Street, Leigh continued periodic trips to the West in search of material that served as inspiration for paintings.

While at Canyon de Chelly during August 1937, Leigh painted a number of small oil studies, mostly 12 x 16 inches, including *Sunset, Canyon de Chelly* (figure 52) and *Moonlight, Canyon de Chelly* (figure 53). In these intimate works, Leigh, who had a fine grasp of color harmony in small landscape studies, discovered the basic essence of Canyon de Chelly. Whether cliffs and cottonwoods bright under the Southwest sun or drenched in moonlight, Leigh

Fig. 52 William R. Leigh, *Sunset, Canyon de Chelly,* 1937. Oil on board, 12 x 16 inches. Gilcrease Museum, Tulsa.

Fig. 53
William R. Leigh, *Moonlight, Canyon de Chelly,* 1937. Oil on board, 12 x 15⅞ inches. Gilcrease Museum, Tulsa.

probed for the canyon's spirit. One of his most famous paintings, *The Lookout* (figure 54), was painted in 1939, when he was seventy-three years old, a result of impressions from his visit to Canyon de Chelly in 1937. In this mural-sized painting, Leigh romanticized the Anasazi of the canyon's past and re-created on canvas the life of prehistoric cliff dwellers as he saw it. Hopi friends from Walpi served as his models for the painting. Part romantic exuberance, part Hiawatha, part Noble Savage, the painting projects Leigh's interpretation of ancient life in the canyon.

Photographer Ansel Adams (1902–1984) first encountered Canyon de Chelly in 1937 on a lengthy trip through New Mexico and Arizona with Georgia O'Keeffe and several other friends. Adams had long coveted the western landscape, starting at age fourteen when he began to spend summers on Sierra Club annual outings at Yosemite National Park. By 1930, the pull of photography and pristine mountain ranges confronted his education as a classical pianist. He attempted to keep both music and photography alive but finally turned from the piano. Thereafter, Adams resolved that photography would mold his destiny, and he quickly emerged as the foremost American landscape photographer of the twentieth century.

In 1941 and 1942, Adams traveled through the West on a commissioned photography project to produce displays for the new Interior building in Washington, D.C., and major national parks. However, owing to war pressures, the project was terminated. Adams arrived at Canyon de Chelly in the autumn of 1941 with a station wagon, sleeping bag, and gasoline stove, slept at night on the rim, then packed his smaller cameras—a 5 x 7 and a miniature—on his back each morning and hiked down steep, faint canyon trails. Sometimes he took a large 8-x-10 camera and explored up the canyon floor with Cozy McSparron, who drove a car outfitted with special tires for sand. One of Adams's best-known photographs, *White House Ruin, Canyon de Chelly* (figure 55), was taken during October 1941. Adams, who admired the work of Timothy O'Sullivan, was unaware until later that he had erected his camera at nearly the identical spot and about the same month, day, and time that O'Sullivan had photographed the ruin in 1873. He returned again in 1947 and took one of his photographs from the rim, the result being *Canyon de Chelly National Monument* (figure 56).

The beauty of Navajo country attracted Gerald Curtis Delano (1890–1972) to Canyon de Chelly in 1943. For nearly twenty years, the canyon, other locations around the sprawling Navajo Reservation, and Navajo people were subjects for Delano's art. Delano grew up in Massachusetts and in January 1910 left to study illustration art at the Art Students League in New York. By the outbreak of World War I, Delano started to sell pen-and-ink illustrations to *Life* magazine, in addition to other commercial assignments. Delano traveled to Denver in the summer of 1919, where he worked at an advertising agency and then on a ranch as a cowboy. For the next several years, he alternated between Colorado and New York. By 1925, his

Fig. 54
William R. Leigh, *The Lookout,* 1939. Oil on canvas, 78 x 128 inches. Woolaroc Museum, Bartlesville, Oklahoma.

Fig. 55
Ansel Adams, *White House Ruin, Canyon de Chelly,* 1941. Photograph. National Archives.

Fig. 56
Ansel Adams, *Canyon de Chelly National Monument,* 1947.
Photograph. National Archives.

paintings had appeared on covers and as illustrations in *Colliers, Cosmopolitan,* and a large array of western pulp-fiction magazines, such as *Frontier Stories, New Western,* and *Ranch Romance.*

After the depression ruined him in 1933, Delano moved to Colorado. He discovered the Navajo and their country in the early 1940s, and they became major themes in his paintings. Canyon de Chelly, in particular, was a favorite destination. He considered one of his paintings, *The Navajo* (figure 57), illustrative of what he felt about the place:

> There is a vastness, an immensity, and a peaceful hush of an enormous cathedral about Arizona's great canyons. Whoever has been within these walls and has seen the flocks of sheep and goats

grazing, heard the distant tinkle of the lead goats bell, listened to the haunting song of the bright-shirted shepherdess, and has seen in the distance an approaching rider, a tiny speck against these massive canyon walls, must yearn to perpetuate his impressions of those precious moments. That is why I paint the canyon and the Navajo. The Navajo people are a proud and beautiful race of great dignity. It is my ideal to show them as I know them. There are fewer poorer people anywhere, yet it would be difficult to find a happier lot, and I wonder if there is not a lesson in this for all of us.

—RICHARD BOWMAN, *Walking with Beauty: The Art and Life of Gerald Curtis Delano*

Delano's works from the 1940s until his death were, in his words, "designed realism." He developed a limited palette, marked by bright colors massed in large areas and stark, bold composition. Delano preferred to make quick, direct sketches of a subject, then used them to develop a final composition in his Denver studio. In *Navajo Sheep* (figure 58) and *Canyon Dwellers* (figure 59), Delano's subjects are integrated with the canyon's mood and organized with quasi-abstract design. Their distinctive colors, primarily purple and blues, endow them with power.

Fig. 58
Gerald Curtis Delano, *Navajo Sheep,* ca. 1944.
Oil on canvas, 20 x 24 inches. Photograph courtesy of Richard G. Bowman.

Fig. 57 (facing)
Gerald Curtis Delano,
The Navajo, ca. 1943. Oil on canvas, 36 x 46 inches. Collection of Mr. and Mrs. Robert L. Mehl. Photograph courtesy of Thomas Nygard, Inc.

Fig. 59
Gerald Curtis Delano, *Canyon Dwellers,* ca. 1945. Oil on canvas, 18 x 20 inches. Photograph courtesy of Richard G. Bowman.

LANDSCAPE OF THE HEART, 1945–PRESENT

After the conclusion of World War II, many American artists turned to a personal imagery, marked by intuitive or improvisational painting and subconscious, invented means. Abstract expressionism soon became the currency by which all painting was judged for several decades. Painters at Canyon de Chelly in the past fifty years have represented such styles as painterly realism, photorealism, pop art, and expressionism. However, each artist's roots are firmly grounded in the varied approaches of American realist landscape painting. With few exceptions, photography during this period has been practiced by artists whose approach to their work includes strict documentation that conveys the light and physical qualities of Canyon de Chelly with economy, clarity, authority, and little ostentation. The painters and photographers who have worked at Canyon de Chelly from the late 1940s to the present are artists linked by a profound, almost religious respect for the canyon's landscapes and rich historical past. Their works are marked by images drawn from the natural world, sometimes heightened, amplified, or exaggerated. In addition, a common thread for these artists is familiarity with the land and concern for craftsmanship and visual content. All of them view Canyon de Chelly with an emphatic sense of wonder.

Gray Bartlett (1885–1951) was born in Rochester, Missouri, and moved with his family to Colorado in 1890. There he worked as a cowboy and at the same time started sketching and painting western scenes. He studied at the Greeley, Colorado Art School, followed by further work at the Art Institute of Chicago. Bartlett was employed as a commercial artist for photoengravers in Denver and later owned an interest in an engraving company. After Bartlett retired in 1937, he moved to Los Angeles, then started to paint again at age fifty-two, having not painted for thirty years.

From a studio in Los Angeles and another at his ranch in Moab, Utah, Bartlett ranged through Arizona, New Mexico, Texas, Utah, and Colorado, and probably visited Canyon de Chelly in 1946 or 1947, where he painted *Canyon of the Pictographs* (figure 60) and *Abode of the Spirits* (see figure 3). They are romantic narratives wherein Bartlett has created a story in the image. All of Bartlett's work included cowboy or Indian figures, set against the backdrop of vivid landscapes.

Between 1919 and 1920, five young artists—Jozef Bakos, Will Shuster, Wladyslaw Mruk, Willard Nash, and Fremont Ellis—settled in Santa Fe, attracted by important artists already there and the stimulation of a vibrant art colony. In 1921, they organized an artists group called *Los Cincos Pintores,* formed for economic and social goals.

Fremont Ellis (1897–1985), born in Virginia City, Montana, was a self-taught artist except for several months at the Art Students League in New York. Love of landscape painting brought him first to El Paso, Texas, then to Santa Fe in 1919. Unable to find a market for his art, he moved to California, then back to Santa Fe in 1921. Before World War II, his paintings and watercolors were patterned after American impressionism—conservative compositions organized around a formula based on bright spots of sunlight contrasted with deep-shadow areas. After the war, Ellis's palette began to brighten and the brush strokes became more fluid. His sun-dappled watercolor *Canyon de Chelly* (figure 61) captured reflections from cliff and sky, the image's mood expressive of canyon life.

Among the great nineteenth-century American landscape painters, there was a credo that painting is a window on the world. If so, Wilson Hurley (b. 1924) portrays landscape in a nineteenth-century luminist style that employs the effect of clear light, challenging artists Albert Bierstadt and Thomas Moran. In his dramatic paintings, which have a mystical affinity for landscape, Hurley uses natural earth colors and

Fig. 60
Gray Bartlett, *Canyon of the Pictographs,* 1946–47. Oil on canvas, 30 x 40 inches. George Stern Fine Arts.

Fig. 61
Fremont Ellis, *Canyon de Chelly,* ca. 1950. Watercolor, 21½ x
27¼ inches. The Gerald Peters Gallery.

structured composition, chooses subject matter in his mind before he finds it, and has a concern for portrayal of what the eye can see on a given day under existing light and cloud conditions.

Hurley first came to Canyon de Chelly in 1971. Another trip to the canyon in 1977 produced *Winter Sunset, de Chelly* (see figure 1). Here, Hurley views the canyon from a perspective of both flying over it and driving along the rim. In this painting, Hurley envisions the canyon's grand sweep, bright under brilliant

Fig. 62
Wilson Hurley, *Anasazi Castle, Canyon del Muerto,* 1980. Oil on canvas, 36 x 60 inches. Photograph courtesy of the artist.

winter sun. Not only are the canyon's sandstone contours exposed by the sun's relentless search for shadowed crevices, but the horizon-line break draws the viewer up and on top of the canyon rim, where Canyon de Chelly merges into the far horizon. He painted a view of Mummy Cave, *Anasazi Castle, Canon del Muerto* (figure 62), in 1980. Hurley and another artist hired a Navajo guide and a four-wheel-drive vehicle to spend a full day in Canyon del Muerto. He painted two small oil studies—one in the morning and the other in late afternoon for light contrast—complemented by photographs made in various lights throughout the day.

Several years later, Hurley painted *Cradleland of the Anasazi* (figure 63) and *Almost Spring, Canon de Chelly, Sliding House Ruins* (figure 64). Both works are reminiscent of nineteenth-century panoramic photography. Hurley re-creates scenes in accurate scale and perspective guided by measurements from Geological Survey contour maps; checks angles, distance, and altitude; then plans perspective from a distance that fits the paintings' dimensions. Both canvases have a romantic sensibility about them, almost Wagnerian, the

Landscape of the Heart, 1945–Present

landscape and ruins being solid and eternal. The canyon is conceptualized into more than mere description and is placed on canvas with serenity and subliminal undertones. There is outspoken fluidity and grace in Hurley's images of Canyon de Chelly—a mythical world, an earthly paradise, presented with technical flair.

Francis H. Beaugureau (b. 1920) frames the great vista of Canyon de Chelly from Spider Rock overlook. In his watercolor *Spider Rock, Canyon de Chelly* (figure 65), he has made a literal transcript of the canyon's configuration, capturing the topographic reality of the landscape as a private mirage.

Born in Chicago, Beaugureau took classes at the Frederic Mizen Academy and the Art Institute of Chicago. Beaugureau spent most of World War II as a B-17 pilot in England and documented the experience with realistic paintings of aircraft in combat. After his discharge from the air force in 1946, he worked as a commercial artist and portrait painter. A thorough technician, Beaugureau's practice is to work in the field armed with a 35mm camera and a bag stuffed with drawing pads and watercolors, then paint on location. He depends on the slides and photographs to assist with documentation of a specific place and to record objective details, while the watercolors recapture the "feel" of a place. His paintings are controlled and carefully executed, with a firm grasp on both detail and serenity.

Fidelity to place, not just anyplace, but a narrowly framed slice of landscape, marks the art of Peter Holbrook (b. 1940). Holbrook's approach to his art is

derived from photo-realism, although he does not consider himself a strict practitioner of that style. An art teacher told him to focus on content first and style would evolve. Holbrook still considers that good advice.

In his Northern California studio, Holbrook paints his work with the assistance of photographs, their projected images a guide for vantage points and detail impossible to capture by other means. Facile in several mediums, Holbrook painted *Canyon de Chelly I* (figure 66) as an oil and acrylic. Although his paintings seem like traditional photo-realist paintings—solid and monolithic—they break into fragmented color and vanish upon close inspection. More sky than earth is the dominant feature that confronts artists who work in the Southwest, but not at Canyon de Chelly where views are often fragmented. As he explores the canyon, Holbrook selects a particular fragment of the rock-dominated landscape, then paints a view of that tightly framed compression. Confronted by Canyon de Chelly's landscapes, Holbrook strives to find meaning in what he sees:

> Canyon de Chelly is nothing if not mysterious. Could this have been the edge of the ocean? A swamp of dinosaurs? How could such dramatic erosion occur in a bone dry desert? Who built these cliff dwellings and where did they disappear to, and why? Even the most mundane questions are elusive: what color is this rock? From buff to blue to maroon, all of it metamorphosing with mineral seepage, age, and changing light conditions. Time perspective, even gravity seems displaced. Value patterns shift in a moment as sheer walls fall into and out of shadow, revealing

Fig. 63
Wilson Hurley, *Cradleland of the Anasazi*, 1985. Oil on canvas, 60 x 48 inches. Photograph courtesy of the artist.

Fig. 64
Wilson Hurley,
Almost Spring,
Canyon de
Chelly, Sliding
House Ruins,
1986. Oil on
canvas, 36 x 66
inches. Photo-
graph courtesy of
the artist.

hieroglyphics of ancient weather patterns. Extraordinary color everywhere; highlights alternately reflecting yellow sun or blue sky; shadows glowing with "bounced" red and orange. Foliage so vividly green it sets up complimentary vibrations. A landscape painter's dream, or nightmare. A place where the traditional conventions are useless and soon abandoned.

—PETER HOLBROOK

Fig. 65
Francis H. Beaugureau, *Spider Rock, Canyon de Chelly,* ca. 1980. Watercolor, 21½ x 29 inches. Collection of John F. Kofron.

Fig. 66 (facing)
Peter Holbrook, *Canyon de Chelly I,* 1981–84. Oil & acrylic on canvas, 56 x 48 inches. Photograph courtesy of the artist.

Fig. 67
Bill Schenck, *Down by the River,* 1992.
Acrylic on canvas, 37 x 41 inches.
Photograph courtesy of the artist.

Bill Schenck (b. 1947) paints images of the modern American West, his subjects being contemporary cowboys, cowgirls, pickups, and Cadillacs—old traditions and new values—done in a flat, simplified manner with the vibrant colors of pop art. Schenck practices a version of abstraction, tempered by use of flattened and stylized images drawn from photographs, a "paint by the numbers" approach. This, along with exaggerated colors, gives his work a distinctive tone.

After periodic trips to Canyon de Chelly in the early and middle 1980s, Schenck began to focus more on the canyon's challenges. He would plan to arrive in early May, when cottonwood leaves had emerged with lucid green color. The image *Down by the River* (figure 67) was painted during a spring visit. Schenck discovered

that the water was still high on the canyon floor and that the Navajo had not yet returned, but he enjoyed painting the effect of water flowing along the canyon streambed as well as long afternoon shadows.

Schenck's experiences at Canyon de Chelly include encounters with remote pastoral scenes. *Canyon Country* (see figure 5) was one of his first attempts to introduce Navajo culture elements into his work. In another canvas, *A Walk to the Water* (figure 68), Schenck decided to paint verdant vegetation patterns with contrast provided by the Navajo woman's velveteen skirt. *A Pink Parasol* (figure 69) seems to capture everything Schenck loves about Canyon de Chelly. A Navajo resident of the canyon, Annie James, stands before the bright sandstone walls, erect under her pink parasol. Schenck considers the painting a perfect

Fig. 68
Bill Schenck, *A Walk to the Water,* 1992. Acrylic on canvas,
48 x 56 inches. Photograph courtesy of the artist.

Fig. 69
Bill Schenck, *A Pink Parasol,* 1992. Acrylic on canvas,
46 x 46 inches. Photograph courtesy of the artist.

Fig. 70
Robert Draper, *Rider,
Canyon de Chelly,* no date.
Watercolor, 11 x 14½
inches. Collection of
Stephen C. Jett.

metaphor for people who still live in the canyon. The woman has conceded some to modern American culture, with her tennis shoes, parasol, and short-hemmed dress, but still retains pride and dignity inherent in Navajo culture. Her mother is the figure in *A Walk to the Water.*

Navajo-Laguna artist Robert D. Draper (b. 1938) has a special affinity for Canyon de Chelly—he was born in Canyon del Muerto. Essentially self-taught, Draper has worked as an art instructor at the Chinle Boarding School and still lives in Chinle. His art has been exhibited at the First Annual American Indian Art Exposition, Heard Museum, Intertribal Indian fairs, New Mexico State Fair, Navajo Tribal Fair, and the Philbrook Art Center, among others. He paints realistic watercolors of the Navajo Reservation landscapes and culture, with Canyon de Chelly being a favorite subject. Draper's watercolor *Rider, Canyon de Chelly* (figure 70) pictures a solitary horseman on the canyon floor, the clear articulation of the image emphasized with muted light and color.

Another Navajo artist, Irving Toddy (b. 1951) works with watercolor and acrylic to document Navajo culture in Canyon de Chelly. The oldest son of famed Navajo artist Beatien Yazz, Toddy attended Utah State University, where he studied

Fig. 71
Irving Toddy, *Crossing the Wash. Canyon de Chelly*, no date. Acrylic & water-color, 17¾ x 16½ inches. Collection of Stephen C. Jett.

painting and illustration. His work has been exhibited at the Santa Fe Indian Market, Gallup Intertribal Indian Fair, Red Cloud Indian School, and the Philbrook Art Center. Toddy, Draper, and several other Navajo painters are known as the Gallup Realists. Their work is a radical departure from traditional Navajo painting. His mixed-media painting, *Crossing the Wash, Canyon de Chelly* (figure 71), is a meticulous image rendered with strict adherence to realism. A Navajo family in their horse-drawn wagon crosses a water-coated wash near Sleeping Duck Rock; their figures, the monolith behind them, and canyon colors are mirrored in the streambed.

Born in Phoenix, Arizona, Ed Mell's roots reach deeply into the state. A passion for illustration led Mell to Art Center College of Design in Los Angeles. After graduation in 1967, he migrated to New York, where he became art director of a large advertising agency. Two years later, he started his own operation, Sagebrush Studios. By this time, his airbrush illustration techniques, particularly his use of angular forms inspired by art deco, had achieved national recognition. But Mell missed the Southwest's open spaces. Restless, he spent the summers of 1971 and 1973 on the Hopi Reservation, where he taught art to Hopi children. Bright skies, faraway horizons, and a Hopi spiritual world convinced him he wanted to be a serious landscape painter. When Mell returned to Phoenix in 1973,

he continued to work in commercial illustration but painted part-time. In 1978, he made the switch to full-time artist.

Mell relishes the visual challenge posed by Canyon de Chelly. On the canyon floor, the wide and far horizon is no longer evident; so Mell responds with a careful selection of particular locales, ones that he photographs and then from which he extracts basic forms for a small oil sketch. *Canyon Cottonwoods* (figure 72), just around the corner from White House Ruin,

Fig. 72
Ed Mell, *Canyon Cottonwoods,* 1994. Oil on canvas, 36 x 36 inches. Photograph courtesy of the artist.

presents a different mood of Canyon de Chelly. A group of cottonwoods are outlined by a dramatic sunset, cliffs behind suffused with a red glow, the nearest wall already darkened. No human figures or presence intrude upon his description of mood; no extraneous details detract from essential shape and line. Another painting, *Chinle Bend* (figure 73), captures the effect of dark clouds over the canyon's luminous geological marvels. Bleached, chromatic cliffs embrace the shallow stream

as it searches various routes through the canyon floor.

Taos artist Barbara Zaring (b. 1947) does not paint the precise optical reality of Canyon de Chelly. A resident of Taos since 1973, Zaring is known for bold, color-filled landscapes. Influenced by Kandinsky, van Gogh, German Expressionists, and the Fauves, Zaring, who considers herself self-taught, lets her creative side guide her painting. This is evident in her Canyon de Chelly work. She prefers to paint large-scale views of

Fig. 73
Ed Mell, *Chinle Bend,* 1994.
Oil on canvas, 48 x 48
inches. Photograph
courtesy of the artist.

Canyon de Chelly that depict a vast area of the canyon, such as *Tsegi Overlook* (figure 74) and *Spider Rock, Whispering Woman* (figure 75)—expansive images marked by vivid color and abstract yet naturalistic forms.

From her home in Arroyo Hondo, New Mexico, a former *morada* built in 1850 as a Penitente place of worship, Alyce Frank (b. 1932) responds to the landscapes of northern New Mexico, the canyonlands of Utah, and Canyon de Chelly. After she and her husband moved to New Mexico in 1962, Frank began

Fig. 74

Barbara Zaring, *Tsegi Overlook,* 1987. Oil on linen, 30 x 40 inches. Photograph courtesy of the artist.

to paint seriously in 1973. Her interest is nurtured by the land's possessive beauty, and remains Frank's primary focus.

The canyon has had an effect on her work as a whole, particularly evidenced by the ever-present use of red on her canvases. Her interest is not variable light or

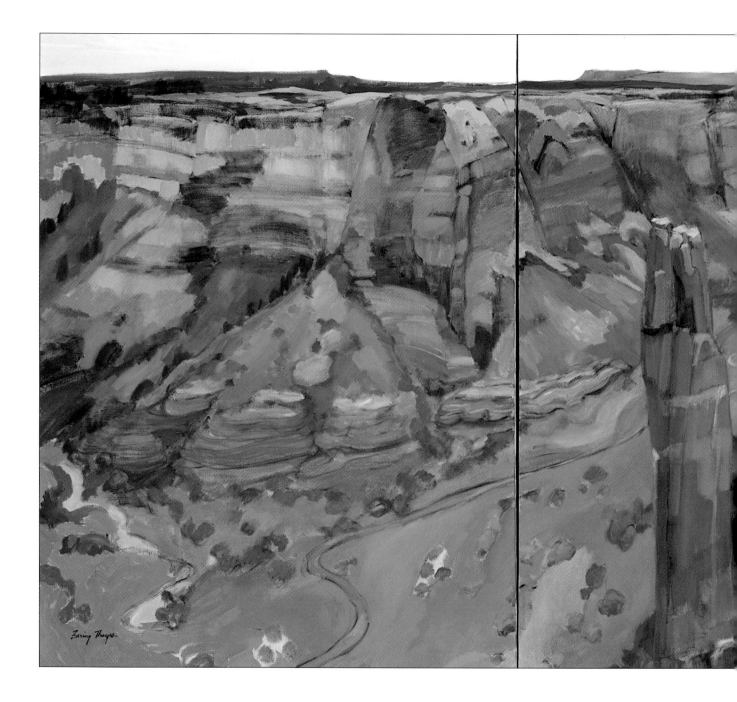

Zaring Thayer

Fig. 75
Barbara Zaring, *Spider Rock, Whispering Woman,* 1994.
Oil on linen, 36 x 48 inches. Photograph courtesy of the artist.

color but is in the scene's basic power. She starts a painting on-site, guided by natural forms that provide a strong framework for her creations. "I will not paint what I see," declares Frank, which releases her from restraints of actual landscape colors. The red ground that permeates sky, mountains, and valleys within her paintings acts to flatten surface areas, while landscape forms are delineated as gestural color shapes, as in *Blade Rock, Canyon de Chelly* (figure 76) and *Ledge House Overlook, Canyon del Muerto* (figure 77).

Fig. 76
Alyce Frank, *Blade Rock, Canyon de Chelly,* 1994.
Oil on linen, 30 x 40 inches. Photograph courtesy of the artist.

Fig. 77
Alyce Frank, *Ledge House Overlook, Canyon del Muerto,* 1994. Oil on linen, 30 x 40 inches. Photograph courtesy of the artist.

Aridity, evolutionary time, spatial patterns, and colors of earth and their consequential changes by time of day and sun position in the sky are elements that drive the art of Merrill Mahaffey (b. 1937). From his home in Santa Fe, Mahaffey searches for monumental forms that enter his canvases in a combination of realism and abstraction, producing an art that responds to landscape as more than scenery. Absorbed by rock formations, water, and desiccated canyons, Mahaffey paints large, powerful canvases devoid of human presence or narrative, primal and timeless in their abstractive yet realistic ability to convey the natural world. Rocks are earth bones and water its lifeblood to Mahaffey, who strives to discover those places that challenge his artistic response.

Mahaffey's painting *Canyon de Chelly, Winter*

Fig. 78
Merrill Mahaffey, *Canyon de Chelly, Winter,* 1994. Acrylic on linen, 46 x 46 inches. Photograph courtesy of the artist.

Fig. 79
Merrill Mahaffey, *Meander Sunset,* 1994. Acrylic on canvas, 46 x 72 inches. Photograph courtesy of the artist.

(figure 78) is a symbolic representation that connects rock and water patterns in the canyon. Reflection of rock on water creates an intriguing mirror of form as discordant parts of the same image. Water, with its own form and colors, seems as much a part of Mahaffey's art as are arid rock and cliff. The water surfaces in Canyon de Chelly's streambed, as Mahaffey has divined it in the painting, are perceived as the canyon's spiritual arteries. In contrast, past and present are joined in *Meander Sunset* (figure 79), where oblique light on shadowed walls creates a tapestry of sensuous beauty.

The vision of Montana artist Charles J. Fritz (b. 1955) is reflected in a meticulous method of realist

Fig. 80
Charles Fritz, *Flying Clouds Over Chinle Wash,* 1994. Oil on canvas, 26 x 30 inches. Photograph courtesy of the artist.

painting based on direct observation of nature and a framework of sound, traditional, and proven artistic principles. Fritz paints idyllic landscapes that focus on the beauty of nature. His paintings convey a harmonious appreciation for the land, an unusual clarity of light, and a sense of specific place. In recognition of his work, Fritz was awarded the prestigious Lee M. Loeb Memorial Award for landscape painting at the 1993 Salmagundi Exhibit in New York.

Fig. 81

Charles Fritz, *Shepherding Where the Walls Tower,* 1994. Oil on canvas, 24 x 16 inches. Photograph courtesy of the artist.

Fritz never tires of distant horizons, moving cloud shadows, and the vaulted sky. After a number of days painting in Canyon de Chelly, Fritz is anxious to see the line where earth meets sky. In *Flying Clouds Over Chinle Wash* (figure 80), he captures broken cloud patterns, high and free over the mouth of Canyon de Chelly where it thrusts into the desert. Fritz's approach to his art stresses pattern, rich color, bold shapes, and the effect of an immense natural world. In response, he searches for locations in the canyon that suggest these combinations. He painted *Shepherding Where the Walls Tower* (figure 81) when an early evening had not yet displaced the sun's play on canyon walls.

Allure of light, the expansive silence of the Southwest's landscapes, and the common symbol of contemporary American life—the highway—are embedded in the art of Woody Gwyn (b. 1944). Born in San Antonio, Texas, Gwyn grew up on the stripped-down landscapes that surrounded Midland, Texas. Gwyn is noted for his contemporary, large-scale landscape paintings that typically include the artifact of a modern interstate or regional high-way—work that embraces relationships between man-made highways set on pristine landscapes.

Gwyn's monotype *Parking Lot, Antelope House* (figure 82) is a metaphor for the reality of late-twentieth-century American culture, for he knows that asphalt pavement is often as much a part of

Fig. 82
Woody Gwyn, *Parking Lot, Antelope House,* 1994. Monotype, 8½ x 11½ inches.
Photograph courtesy of the artist.

landscapes as are sublime views. About a hundred feet from the parking lot—down another nine hundred feet—and eight hundred years away lies Antelope House. The image seems like an Anasazi painting, with yellow stripes arranged in precise yet abstract fashion on a laid-down wall—the parking lot, modern culture's version of ancient symbols. What Gwyn has offered is a message that the past and nature have receded from view.

For Lindsay Holt II (b. 1958), the Southwest landscape is full of symbolic meaning. He is drawn by a feeling of timelessness in the locations he explores, their essence being inspiration for his work. Consequently, his painting has evolved as a personal vision quest—a revelation of spirit, or some sense of truth—for unique places and precise moments in time. Holt was born in El Paso, Texas, and after graduation from Los Angeles's Art Center College of Design in 1982, returned to his birthplace. After several years, he migrated to Abiquiu, New Mexico, then to Santa Fe in 1992. Sources for Holt's inspiration come from the Southwest's natural light and distinctive landscapes, in particular, those of northern New Mexico. This passion for the natural world flows through and into his work, where reference to present environmental conditions may be implicit yet illusive.

Where Monument Canyon joins Canyon de Chelly, ponderosa pine dot the rim areas. Holt's painting *Ponderosa, Canyon de Chelly* (figure 83) presents a view of several trees high along the edge of a cliff in Monument Canyon. One tree has pioneered a foothold on a small, light-illuminated ledge jutting from a fissure. Lyrical light from the canyon floor flickers on the shadowed cliff. While the painting is drawn from evocation of place, the image is more a landscape of the mind.

Serene places, sanctuaries of nature and culture, are the images painter Brooks Anderson (b. 1957) seeks. Anderson travels through the American West in a search for inspiration from the face of the land. His romantic landscapes are compared to Maxfield Parrish's, but rooted in a specific place. Influenced by painter Richard Diebenkorn, among others, Anderson's paintings contain spiritual currents, not only of the landscapes he paints but of the manner in which they should be painted.

Fig. 83
Lindsay Holt II, *Ponderosa, Canyon de Chelly,* 1994. Oil on stretched paper, 45 x 30 inches. Photograph courtesy of the artist.

Anderson's impressions are ones of tranquility and grandeur; his feel for Canyon de Chelly runs as deeply as the sandstone walls. As he pauses before the canyon, Anderson feels honor, respect, and humility, embraced by the warm walls that have sustained an ancient civilization. The incentive for his painting *Many Farms* (figure 84) was the result of abstract impressions—the interplay of diagonal, spiral movement of canyon walls and early morning light that bathes the generations-held Navajo farm lying far below Junction Ruin Overlook. The painting suggests a thoughtful regard for the canyon's natural and human solitude.

Tucson artist Lynn Taber-Borcherdt's (b. 1943) paintings reflect influence from the desert's immense scale that has led her to focus inward in search of balance between landscapes and her own thoughts about existence. When Taber-Borcherdt visits Can-

Fig. 84
Brooks Anderson, *Many Farms,* 1994. Pastel, 9½ x 12½ inches. Photograph courtesy of the artist.

Fig. 85
Lynn Taber-Borcherdt, *For Long Periods of Time,* 1994. Alkyd on masonite, 32 x 40 inches. Photograph by Robin Stancliff.

yon de Chelly, she is captivated by spectacular cloud formations and sunsets. In *For Long Periods of Time* (figure 85), a departing sun converts canyon walls into apparitions. The painting seems mysterious, the landscape enhanced by unearthly twilight. That same celestial, melancholy light pulsates through her pastel, *At This Point in Time* (figure 86). Her landscapes, almost monochromatic with subtle and rich tonality, convey another aspect of the canyon's mood: quiet, enchanted, enigmatic, haunted. They are Taber-Borcherdt's subconscious vocabulary drawn from her love of drama and magic. The canyon's immense, timeless space is a companion for her art.

Fig. 86
Lynn Taber-Borcherdt, *At This Point in Time,* 1994.
Pastel on paper, 18 x 22 inches. Photograph by Robin Stancliff.

Every landscape painter and photographer knows that his or her selection of view or subject is a chosen fragment and that landscape reality extends well beyond the canvas or photographic print. Within the rich and varied history of painting and photography at Canyon de Chelly lies the artist's preconceived approach to painting or photography, that varied self-conscious rationalization through which all, from Richard Kern to contemporary ones, have defined the canyon's landscapes and native peoples.

Artists at Canyon de Chelly have been, and continue to be, enthralled with just what might lie around the next bend on the canyon floor or what great vistas unfold from different locations on the rims. All have reacted with delight, close observation, and reverence. Canyon de Chelly's early visual history is one primarily concerned with photography as various scientific groups probed the canyon's myriad wonders. Most pioneer photographers' reactions were those concerned with strict observational transcripts of nature, as embodied by their images of prehistoric ruins, Navajo inhabitants, and massive, elemental walls that seem to have a life of their own.

As the twentieth century began, painters contributed their interpretations to the visual recognition of Canyon de Chelly. What they added to the palette was color—and attempts to conceptualize the canyon into something beyond strict description. While the smell and form of the land still remained, their work increasingly used a new vocabulary to express reactions to the canyon's empirical reality. During the 1920s and 1930s, painters, responding to conflict between the world of nature and increased American urbanization, filled their canvases with a sense of serenity and oneness

Photographer unknown, *Canyon del Muerto,* 1902, Maynard Dixon on horse. Collection of Becky Jenkins.

with the canyon's environment.

Photography underwent changes in the early twentieth century, as photographers, influenced by new art traditions, turned to pictorialist methods. These artists, in effect, tried to find romantic reality beyond actuality as they manipulated prints, posed subjects, or otherwise experimented with visual conceptions. For photographers such as Edward S. Curtis and Roland Reed, the canyon's landscapes were of lesser importance as they used their photographic techniques to capture and even to relive what they thought were vanishing lifeways of the American Indian.

After World War II, painters and photographers continued to visualize Canyon de Chelly as solid and eternal, a place of solace and escape from pressures of modern American culture. Many contemporary artists represented in this book have chosen a path to humanistic principles, even perhaps a regenerated spirit of romanticism. Most share similar inclinations and traits, and, while artistic styles vary, they probe similar trails. Their art, as has been the case from the Anasazi universe to the present, are windows into Canyon de Chelly's world.

Initial impressions of Canyon de Chelly led to the belief that this is a place where time has stopped. But time, or time's result, continues. Serious erosion along the streambed has threatened parts of Canyon de Chelly's floodplain and alluvial terraces. Second canyons laid down in the original canyon are forming, menacing agriculture and access. According to a Navajo legend, if level ground on the canyon floor should become an open abyss, it would be the end of man. Navajo traditions in the canyon are eroding as well. Sheep raising is in decline, and young Navajo prefer to work in Chinle or elsewhere. Development crowds

monument boundaries, and power lines mar landscapes near the rim areas. Trash and graffiti pose serious concerns for National Park Service and Navajo government officials. One painter remarked that he had to clear mounds of trash away before he could erect his easel. As he painted, he contested space with passing pickups, their radios blasting away the canyon's solitude with rock music. Even in remote side canyons, reserves of wildlife and native vegetation are shrinking as human intrusion intensifies.

Yet the landscapes and cultural history of Canyon de Chelly retain an ability to convey emotions through art, the canyon's diversity of moods offering solace, reassurance, and replenishment. The spiritual continues to be manifested in Canyon de Chelly's monumental landscapes, much as the early artists certainly must have encountered it in the nineteenth century. A landscape of fragile, elemental beauty, Canyon de Chelly remains a shrine for painters and photographers, a place of myth and poetry, a place of vanished and successive cultures, a landscape of the heart.

BIBLIOGRAPHY

BOOKS

Bowman, Richard C. *Walking With Beauty: The Art and Life of Gerald Curtis Delano.* Denver: Privately printed, 1990.

Broder, Patricia Janis. *Shadows on Glass: The Indian World of Ben Wittick.* Savage, Maryland: Rowman and Littlefield, 1990.

Casagrande, Louis B., and Phillips Bourns. *Side Trips: The Photography of Sumner W. Matteson, 1898–1908.* Milwaukee: Milwaukee Public Museum and Science Museum of Minnesota, 1983.

Cather, Willa. *The Professor's House.* New York: Alfred A. Knopf, 1925.

Coen, Rena Neumann. *The Paynes: Edgar and Elsie, American Artists.* Minneapolis: Payne Studios, 1988.

Davis, Barbara A., and Edward S. Curtis. *The Life and Times of a Shadow Catcher.* San Francisco: Chronicle Books, 1985.

DuBois, June. *W. R. Leigh: The Definitive Illustrated Biography.* Kansas City: The Lowell Press, 1977.

Forrest, Earl L. "Louis Akin: Artist of Old Arizona." In *Westerners Brand Book.* Vol. 6. Los Angeles: Los Angeles Corral of the Westerners, 1956.

Fowler, Don D. *Myself in the Water: The Western Photographs of John K. Hillers.* Washington, D.C.: Smithsonian Institution Press, 1989.

Garman, Ed. *Raymond Jonson, Painter.* Albuquerque: University of New Mexico Press, 1976.

Grant, Campbell. *Canyon de Chelly: Its People and Rock Art.* Tucson: University of Arizona Press, 1978.

Guide to Southwestern National Monuments. Popular Series, no 1. Coolidge, Arizona: Southwestern Monuments Association, December 1938.

Hagerty, Donald J. *Desert Dreams: The Art and Life of Maynard Dixon.* Layton, Utah: Gibbs Smith, Publisher, 1993.

Hammond, George P., ed. *Campaigns in the West 1856–1861: The Journal and Letters of Colonel John van Duesen DuBois with Pencil Sketches by Joseph Heger.* Tucson: Arizona Historical Society, 1949.

Laird, Helen. *Carl Oscar Borg and Magic Region.* Layton, Utah: Gibbs M. Smith, Inc., 1986.

Mahood, Ruth, ed. *Photographer of the Southwest: Adam Clark Vroman.* Los Angeles: Ward Ritchie Press, 1961.

McNitt, Frank, ed. *Navajo Expedition: Journal of a Military Reconnaissance From Santa Fe, New Mexico to the Navajo Country, Made in 1849 by Lieutenant James Hervey Simpson.* Norman: University of Oklahoma Press, 1964.

Naef, Weston, in collaboration with James N. Wood. *Era of Exploration: The Rise of Landscape Photography in the American West, 1860–1885.* Buffalo, New York: Albright-Knox Art Gallery/New York: The Metropolitan Museum of Art, 1975.

On Desert Trails With Everett Ruess. El Centro: Desert Magazine Press, 1940.

Rusho, W. L. *Everett Ruess: A Vagabond For Beauty.* Salt Lake City: Gibbs M. Smith, 1983.

Sacks, Peter. *Woody Gwyn.* Lubbock: Texas Tech University Press, 1995.

Seavey, Kent L. *Francis John McComas (1875–1938).* San Francisco: California Historical Society, 1965.

Snyder, Joel. *American Frontiers: The Photographs of Timothy O'Sullivan, 1867–1874.* Millerton, New York: Aperture, 1981.

Weber, David J. *Richard H. Kern: Expeditionary Artist in the Far West, 1848–1853.* Albuquerque: University of New Mexico Press, 1985.

Wilson Hurley: A Retrospective Exhibition. Kansas City: Lowell Press/The Albuquerque Museum/Buffalo Bill Historical Center, 1985.

PERIODICALS

Allen, Scott Douglas. "Brooks Anderson." *Arts Magazine* 60 (April 1986): 110.

"Bartlett-Painter." *Arizona Highways* (August 1945): 67–68.

Cuba, Stanley L. "Merrill Mahaffey." *Southwest Art* (September 1992): 70–76.

Curtis, Edward S. "Vanishing Indian Types: The Tribes of the Southwest." *Scribner's Magazine* 34 (May 1906): 513–529.

Dixon, Maynard. "Red Walls of Navajoland." *Arizona Highways* 14 (June 1943): 45.

Gillispie, Nancy. "Barbara Zaring Thayer." *Southwest Art* (September 1989): 64–69.

Gish-Reich, Shirley, and Dr. Sheldon Reich. "Francis Beaugureau: Adventures Recaptured." *Southwest Art* (February 1984): 73–79.

Goodwin, Martha Burnett. "Alyce Frank." *Southwest Art* (November 1991): 70–76.

Hagerty, Donald J. "Reflection Made Visible: The Art of Ed Mell." *Arizona Highways* (July 1985): 40–45.

Johnston, Patricia Condon. "The Indian Photographs of Roland Reed." *The American West* 2 (1978): 44–57.

Pyne, Lynn. "Bill Schenck." *Southwest Art* (October 1990): 126–33.

Whipple, Barbara. "Peter Holbrook." *American Artist* 48 (March 1984): 60–65, 77–79.